Getting Skills Right

Improving the Quality of Non-Formal Adult Learning

LEARNING FROM EUROPEAN BEST PRACTICES ON QUALITY ASSURANCE

BETTER POLICIES FOR BETTER LIVES

This work is published under the responsibility of the Secretary-General of the OECD. The opinions expressed and arguments employed herein do not necessarily reflect the official views of OECD member countries.

This document, as well as any data and map included herein, are without prejudice to the status of or sovereignty over any territory, to the delimitation of international frontiers and boundaries and to the name of any territory, city or area.

The statistical data for Israel are supplied by and under the responsibility of the relevant Israeli authorities. The use of such data by the OECD is without prejudice to the status of the Golan Heights, East Jerusalem and Israeli settlements in the West Bank under the terms of international law.

Please cite this publication as:
OECD (2021), *Improving the Quality of Non-Formal Adult Learning: Learning from European Best Practices on Quality Assurance*, Getting Skills Right, OECD Publishing, Paris, *https://doi.org/10.1787/f1b450e1-en*.

ISBN 978-92-64-91963-1 (print)
ISBN 978-92-64-35666-5 (pdf)

Getting Skills Right
ISSN 2520-6117 (print)
ISSN 2520-6125 (online)

Foreword

The world of work is changing. Digitalisation, globalisation, and population ageing are having a profound impact on the type and quality of jobs that are available and the skills required to perform them. The extent to which individuals, firms and economies can reap the benefits of these changes will depend critically on the readiness of adult learning systems to help people develop and maintain relevant skills over their working careers.

High quality is essential to ensure that the resources devoted to training programmes help workers to keep their skills relevant in a changing world of work. This report addresses the crucial question of how quality can be ensured in the field of adult learning. It provides an overview of quality assurance systems across Europe, highlighting their implementation features, governance structures and success factors. In particular, the report focuses on non-formal adult learning, which is "institutionalised, intentional and planned by an education provider" outside of the formal education sector and which does not lead to a formal qualification recognised by the national or sub-national education authorities.

The report is structured around five chapters. Chapter 1 provides some background information necessary to put the study into context, including definitions of the main concepts under scrutiny and the challenges faced by institutions in setting up quality assurance systems for adult education. Common tools used to ensure quality in adult training across European countries are then examined and carefully detailed, distinguishing between those imposing minimum quality requirements on providers (such as quality labels in Chapter 2) and those relying on less strict requirements (e.g. self-evaluations in Chapter 3). The importance of adopting a wider, holistic approach to quality in adult education is emphasised in Chapter 4, with a discussion of the role played by additional support structures, such as the validation of prior learning, the professionalisation of the teaching staff, and the involvement of the social partners. Chapter 5 concludes, proposing a decision tree to help authorities identify what are the main areas of discussion and action to develop a quality assurance system for non-formal adult learning.

This report was prepared by Michele Tuccio from the Directorate for Employment, Labour and Social Affairs, under the supervision of Glenda Quintini (Skills team manager) and Mark Keese (Head of the Skills and Employability Division). Useful comments were provided by Stefano Scarpetta and Julie Lassébie (OECD), Patricia Perez-Gomez and Claudia Piferi (DG REFORM, European Commission), and Antonio Ranieri and Ernesto Villalba (Cedefop). The OECD Secretariat would also like to acknowledge valuable feedback on the report by staff at the Dutch Ministry of Education, Culture and Science and at the Public Service of Wallonia.

This report is published under the responsibility of the Secretary General of the OECD, with the financial assistance of the European Union via the Structural Reform Support Programme. The views expressed in this report should not be taken to reflect the official position of OECD member countries nor the official position of the European Union.

Table of contents

FIGURES

TABLES

Follow OECD Publications on:

http://twitter.com/OECD_Pubs

http://www.facebook.com/OECDPublications

http://www.linkedin.com/groups/OECD-Publications-4645871

http://www.youtube.com/oecdilibrary

http://www.oecd.org/oecddirect/

Acronyms and abbreviations

ANFOR	French Standardisation Association
ANQEP	Portuguese National Agency for Qualification and Vocational Education
ANSI	American National Standards Institute
BSI	British Standards Institution
CEDEFOP	European Centre for the Development of Vocational Training
CNEFOP	French National Council for Employment, Training and Vocational Guidance
COFRAC	French Accreditation Committee
CPF	French Personal Training Account
CQAF	Common Quality Assurance Framework
ECVET	European Credit System for Vocational Education and Training
EFQM	European Foundation for Quality Management
ENQAVET	European Network on Quality Assurance in Vocational Education and Training
EQARF	European Quality Assurance Reference Framework for Vocational Education and Training
EQAVET	European Quality Assurance Reference Framework for Vocational Education and Training
EQF	European Qualifications Framework
EU	European Union
FINEEC	Finnish Education Evaluation Centre
IAG	Information, Advice and Guidance
ISO	International Organization for Standardization
KSQA	Korean Skills Quality Authority
LQW	Learner-Oriented Quality Certification for Further Education Organizations
OECD	Organisation for Economic Cooperation and Development
OFSTED	Office for Standards in Education, Children's Services and Skills
OQEA	Offering Quality Education to Adults
NGO	Non-governmental organisation
NQF	National Qualifications Frameworks
NRTO	Dutch Council for Education and Training
PAIDEIA	Action Plan for Innovation in Adult Learning
RNCQ	French national quality reference system for adult training
SAS	Swiss Accreditation Service
SRSP	Structural Reform Support Programme
SVEB	Swiss Federation for Adult Learning
TWG	Thematic Working Group
VAE	French Validation of Prior Experience
VET	Vocational Education and Training
WBA	Austrian Academy of Continuing Education

Executive summary

A confluence of global megatrends such as globalisation, technological progress and population ageing are changing the types of jobs that are available and the skills required to perform them. Many analysts argue that the COVID-19 crisis has accelerated these changes, especially in the area of digitalisation and the adoption of new technologies. In this context, more than ever adult learning plays a crucial role in helping workers to update their skills and acquire new ones in order to match labour market needs. This is particularly important for adults with low skills. Not only are low-skilled jobs at high risk of being automated, but many of the emerging occupations require high-level cognitive skills. The potential benefits of adult training are numerous and include greater employability and access to better quality jobs, increased productivity, improved civic participation, and – most importantly – a greater sense of individual fulfilment and well-being.

Yet, in order to achieve these positive gains, education and training needs to be of high quality and ensure successful learning outcomes for all participants. In the context of tight public and private budgets following the COVID-19 emergency, guaranteeing quality provision of training will become even more important to ensure that investments in training provide value for money. Quality provision is also seen as a key tool to create trust in the adult training system, especially for non-formal training, as well as a marker of prestige and credibility for providers. Whether their funding is private or public, providers' efforts towards greater training quality help them remain accountable to their stakeholders and students. Overall, a culture of continuous programme improvement contributes to promoting providers' future performance and creating a virtuous circle in the whole education and training sector.

This report addresses the crucial question of how quality can be enhanced in the field of adult learning. It provides an overview of quality assurance systems across Europe, highlighting their implementation features, governance structures and success factors. In particular, the study focuses on non-formal adult learning, which is "institutionalised, intentional and planned by an education provider" outside of the formal education sector and which does not lead to a formal qualification that is recognised by the national or sub-national education authorities. In fact, compared to formal education – which is supervised by national or sub-national governments – non-formal learning is typically less regulated, and its quality remains highly variable, not only across countries but across providers within a country. At the same time, in all OECD countries, non-formal training plays a leading role for upskilling adults, in particular those with low levels of skills, who are usually reluctant to enter a formal education pathway. In any given year, about 40% of adults participate in at least one non-formal training activity, compared with just 8% engaging in formal training.

The report shows that the landscape of quality assurance systems in non-formal adult learning varies considerably. Overall, it is possible to identify three approaches to quality assurance:

1. The *regulatory approach* imposes minimum quality requirements that providers need to meet in order to be allowed to operate or access public funds;
2. The *advisory approach* uses guidelines and examples of good practices to inspire providers engaging in quality development efforts;
3. The *organic approach* leaves it completely to providers to define their own quality needs.

To operationalise these approaches, two categories of quality assurance tools seem to prevail in the European context: quality certificates and labels, and (self-)evaluations. Quality certificates and labels impose minimum requirements that training providers need to fulfil in order to be certified, with the objective of guaranteeing a standard, uniform level of quality of services. Evaluations – done either by providers themselves or by external bodies – aim at assessing the current quality of training through subjective measures of satisfaction with training or objective measures of training processes and outcomes, with the ultimate goal of setting up a plan to improve it in the near future, if necessary.

Given their nature, quality certificates and labels are mostly used by countries following a *regulatory approach* to quality assurance. These tools have the potential of guaranteeing consistently good quality training services, ensuring customers' protection and satisfaction by providing them with straightforward, standardised information about providers' quality. However, their ability to correct market failures associated with asymmetries of information is effective only if the information conveyed is valuable, credible and accurate. If labels are not perceived as reliable by the wider public, they can only have a marginal or even counterproductive impact. Quality labels and certificates are also costly for providers, both in terms of money and time, and they become of little value if they encounter resistance to change from within the business.

In contrast to labels and certificates, evaluations – especially self-evaluations – may help create a longer-lasting quality culture, by ensuring that providers internalise the rationale for putting in place quality efforts. For this reason, evaluations have been widely used in countries with an *advisory approach* to quality, whose core is really to create a bottom-up, self-standing interest of providers in quality improvements. Yet, this feature of evaluation is particularly important also when countries adopt a *regulatory approach* to quality assurance, to ensure that organisations do not think their actions towards quality improvements should end after obtaining a certificate. Quality assurance is an ongoing, dynamic process, since there is always something to improve. The drawback of self-evaluations, however, is that both governments and prospective learners have no assurance of getting good-quality services, but must partly rely on trust in the providers, especially when evaluations' results are not published on a regular and comparable basis across providers. Moreover, it typically takes some time for quality assurance systems based on (self-) evaluations to produce some quality improvements, which can create a sense of the futility of this approach in providers.

This report also stresses the importance of establishing a wide and holistic quality approach, where typical quality assurance tools – such as certification and evaluations – are complemented with additional support structures. Some of the most frequent support initiatives are reviewed: provision of support for the validation of prior learning and lifelong guidance, professionalisation of teaching staff, involvement of social partners, but also provision of best practices and guidelines and consumer protection in terms of publication of information on quality.

1 Setting the scene

While virtually all formal adult education programmes have some sort of quality assurance mechanisms, quality assurance in non-formal training is rare and more scattered. In most countries, the sector defines its own professional standards (*organic approach*). However, following some internal or external pressures, the authorities may decide to intervene, thereby facing the choice between imposing minimum quality requirements for providers to operate or access public funds (*regulatory approach*) and just advising providers on how to best improve their quality (*advisory approach*). Two sets of tools are typically used to demonstrate quality: quality certificates and labels, and (self-)evaluations.

The challenges of ensuring quality in non-formal adult learning

Given the abstract nature of the term "quality", definitions are scattered throughout the education literature. To promote a common understanding, the European Centre for the Development of Vocational Training (Cedefop) of the European Union created a glossary in 2011 on the terminologies used for quality in education and training. Quality is defined as "all characteristics of an entity that bear on its ability to satisfy stated and implied needs" or "the degree to which a set of inherent characteristics fulfils requirements" (Cedefop, 2011[1]). The safeguard of quality has been labelled quality assurance, that represents all "activities involving planning, implementation, evaluation, reporting, and quality improvement, implemented to ensure that all education and training (content of programmes, curricula, assessment and validation of learning outcomes, etc.) meet the quality requirements expected by stakeholders" (Cedefop, 2011[1]). Although related, quality assurance and quality control do not coincide and should not be confused: quality assurance focuses on making sure that the processes to achieve certain results are of high quality, while quality control focuses on the end result itself.

Despite being often characterised by different sector-based regimes, all *formal* adult education programmes generally have a quality component (Broek and Buiskool, 2013[2]), be it in the form of self-evaluations, external evaluations, or the adoption of existing quality systems (such as ISO standards). Furthermore, the European Union and its institutions have been quite active in developing quality standards and guidelines in higher education and vocation training during the past few years. For example, in 2009 the European Parliament approved the European Quality Assurance Reference Framework for VET (EQAVET) in order to ensure quality of VET provision, while the Standards and Guidelines for Quality Assurance in the European Higher Education Area have been adopted in 2005 and recently revised in 2015 (for more details on the European Union approaches to quality assurance in continuing adult education see Box 1.1).

In contrast, defining in a standardised way the concept of quality in *non-formal* adult education has proved to be very challenging – let alone assuring quality throughout the whole sector. As a result, quality assurance mechanisms in non-formal training differ from country to country, and how quality is achieved and monitored can be very different (Prisăcariu, 2014[3]). Very often, countries do not have any national-level quality framework in place for non-formal training. When they do, these quality frameworks typically emanate from bottom-up initiatives by the providers themselves.

Why is it harder for governments to set up quality assurance mechanisms for non-formal training? Part of the explanation lies in the costs (both financial and not) of such mechanisms. In fact, quality assurance often requires both financial and human resources that providers of non-formal training might not have. Compared to formal education, the time spent on course planning and implementation in non-formal training is also much shorter or varied, making it sometimes challenging to adopt quality assurance mechanisms. Moreover, while by its very nature formal education fully embraces inspections and compliance with rules, non-formal training providers tend to shy away from bureaucracy (Latchem, 2012[4]). There might also be some resistance from formal operators in allowing a more formalised certification of the quality of their non-formal and informal competitors.

Another significant obstacle to the development of a national quality assurance framework in non-formal adult training is the fragmentation of the numerous different approaches to quality of the sector itself (European Commission, 2013[5]). Such a diverse landscape makes it difficult to stimulate quality development, especially in countries where governance is highly decentralised. In fact, whilst in several European countries policies for adult learning are set at national level, responsibilities can be decentralised to regional and local levels, as is the case for example in Austria, France, Denmark, Sweden, Norway and the Netherlands. Other important challenges to the development of quality assurance in non-formal adult education are linked to the lack of monitoring data essential to understand the participation and learning outcomes of students, and the limited availability of validation of prior learning and lifelong guidance, which are central to the quality of adult education since they enable access, participation and progression.

Mapping quality assurance approaches and tools in adult training

In spite of these challenges, several European countries have put in place initiatives to improve the quality of their non-formal adult education sectors. Adapting the framework by Hooley and Rice (2019[6]), from a theoretical point of view the various efforts can be grouped into three approaches: (1) the *regulatory approach* typically sets out clear minimum quality requirements that providers need to meet in order to be recognised; (2) the *advisory approach* advises providers on what quality should look like, providing guidelines and examples of good practices for them to follow; and (3) the *organic approach* leaves to providers the overall definition of their own professional standards and quality systems. Before going into details on each framework, it is important to stress that, while theoretically different, these three approaches to quality assurance are not always clear-cut and they can co-exist in some countries.

In practice, quality assurance in all countries starts – either deliberately or unintentionally by not taking any explicit stance on the matter – from an *organic approach*, allowing providers to completely self-manage their quality without even providing a common definition of quality in adult education. At a certain point, internal demands by policy makers or external pressures from, for example, civil society and NGOs may call for the harmonization and steady development of the quality of training provision across the whole sector. At that point, public authorities face the choice between imposing certain minimum quality requirements for providers to operate or access public funds (the *regulatory approach*) and just advising providers on how to best improve their quality (the *advisory approach*). Clearly, the trade-off between these two paradigms is that the latter leaves more room for providers to best find their own paths to quality while the former allows ensuring a minimum, more uniform level of quality across the sector.

The choice between the two approaches typically depends on the motivations that induced the authorities to develop a quality assurance mechanism in first place – with stronger pressures typically leading to the stricter *regulatory approach*. In addition, there are other two reasons for why, over past years, certain countries have preferred non-binding evaluations to binding certifications. On the one hand, the adult training market may not be mature enough to be subject to external quality requirements, which, if enforced, would probably crowd out most of the existing providers. On the other hand, in certain contexts there may be no need to impose quality disclosure through certifications since organisations may have incentives to voluntarily disclose quality. This is the case, for example, when most providers in the market consider their services to be of good quality and henceforth willingly publicize their quality information. In these circumstances, all providers are compelled to disclose their quality since, in the absence of disclosed information, consumers could infer that the organisation is concealing poor quality (Grossman, 1981[7]). In both cases – the training market not mature enough or widespread voluntary disclosure of quality information – self-evaluations are the typical tool to signal quality in *advisory approaches*.

Once countries have decided to move away from an *organic approach* and have made the choice between following the *regulatory* or *advisory* approach, they need to select the appropriate tools to foster a quality culture (Figure 1.1). The most used tools throughout the OECD area are certifications and quality labels, evaluations by an external body and self-evaluations by providers. Furthermore, countries have put in place a whole plethora of additional support structures aimed at helping non-formal training institutions improve their overall quality.

Certification is the "process by which a third party gives written assurance that a product, process or service conforms to specified requirements" (Cedefop, 2011[11]), and aim at attesting that relevant quality actions are conducted.[1] Providers of adult training need to meet certain minimum quality standards in order to be certified, thereby ensuring that customers are offered effective and efficient training. In addition, other strengths of the certification framework include the fact that it represents an evaluation tool to providers themselves, as well as a monitoring tool for policy makers. To indicate that compliance with standards has been verified, countries also often rely on quality labels. Since labels are a form of communication targeted directly to the end consumer, to be effective and meaningful they not only need to be backed up by a good certification system without conflicts of interest, but the system must also be transparent, information on the content and the organisation behind the label must be accessible, and the meaning of the label must be consistent across all bodies carrying it. In light of such transparency, many European countries have made certification and quality labels compulsory in order to receive public funding.[2] As it appears clear, certifications and quality labels are used only in the *regulatory approach*.

At the opposite side of the spectrum are self-evaluations by providers. Based on public, general guidelines, national and international best practices, and common standards of the sector, this tool helps providers develop their quality by self-assessing the current value of their training services and setting up a plan to improve it in the near future. Self-evaluations are commonly used by countries adopting an *advisory approach* to quality assurance, since they allow for a great flexibility and low levels of external control (but not always, as is the case in few European countries, where self-evaluations is compulsory in order to receive public funds). In contrast, evaluations by external bodies lie somewhere in the middle. In fact, they are typically based on precise guidelines, but they do not entail fixed minimum quality requirements and targets, thereby leaving more discretion to the evaluation body to assess providers' quality levels. External evaluations are usually tied to rights to operate or access to public funding (like in the *regulatory approach*). Although seemingly less demanding than certifications and quality labels for providers, the evaluation of the quality of training programmes and providers can be a challenging task, as evaluation exercises require information on many different aspects. Effectiveness of training is generally measured by looking at training outcomes, such as labour market entry, or satisfaction with the provided training. These outcomes can be assessed through a variety of monitoring and evaluation methods, including audits, on-site inspections, and reports.

Figure 1.1. Evolution of approaches and tools for quality assurance in non-formal adult education

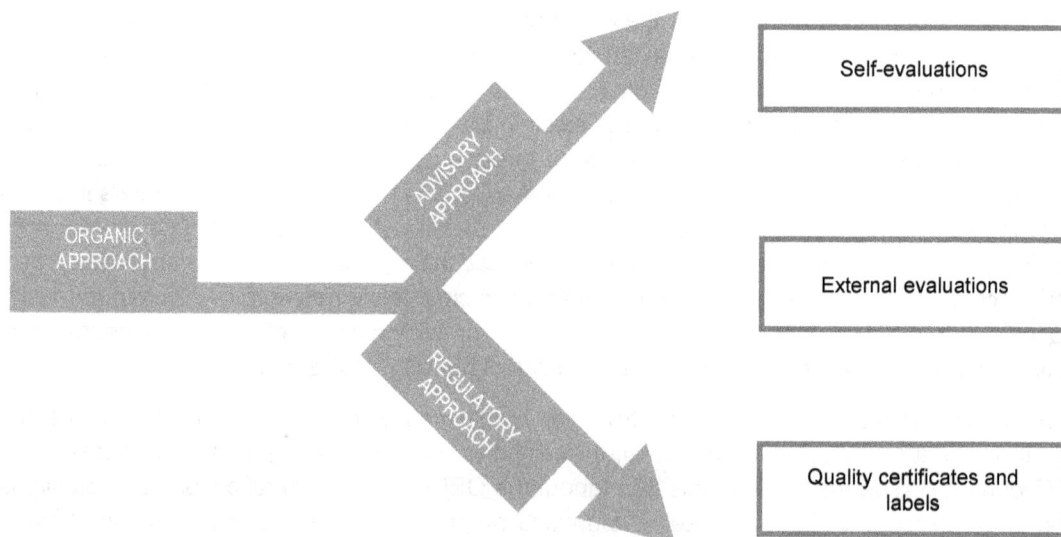

Box 1.1. EU approaches to quality assurance in adult education

To strengthen the common European labour market and build equitable, sustainable and knowledge-based societies, over the past two decades a series of recommendations and initiatives have been developed at the EU level to help member countries move towards a model of quality adult training. This box briefly reviews the major milestones from 2000 to nowadays (Table 1.1).

At the turn of the millennium, the so-called *Lisbon Strategy 2000-10* was one of the seminal EU initiatives recommending greater investments in adult learning with the ultimate goal of upskilling and improving both economic development and social inclusion. At the same time, the European Commission funded the *European Forum on Quality in VET* as a platform for collaboration between Member countries, the social partners and the European Commission in the area of quality assurance in vocational education and training (VET). The forum developed a work programme for 2001-02, focusing on four central areas: (1) quality management approaches for VET providers; (2) self-assessment in VET institutions; (3) types of examination and certification practices; and (4) indicators for a European quality in VET strategy.

To facilitate access to lifelong learning, the 2002 *Copenhagen Declaration* acknowledged the importance of transparency, comparability, transferability, and recognition of competences and qualifications between different countries. The development of reference levels, common principles for certification, and common measures, including a credit transfer system for vocational education and training, was recommended. In this context, the *Common Quality Assurance Framework* (CQAF) for vocational education and training was developed in 2004. CQAF was a quality management framework based on best practices from Member States and aimed at serving as a reference for the development of quality in national VET systems by describing basic principles, criteria and instruments for the implementation of quality assurance processes.

The following year, the European Commission established the *European Network on Quality Assurance in VET* (ENQAVET) in order to provide a sustainable platform to support the implementation of the Copenhagen Declaration. In particular, ENQAVET attempted to develop a culture of quality assurance and continuous improvements across the EU and common guidelines for the development of quality assurance in VET systems.

Building on these initial EU initiatives, in 2008 the European Parliament and the Council of the European Union adopted a recommendation establishing the *European Qualifications Framework* (EQF), a framework encompassing all education and training qualifications. All member states were encourage to link their national qualification systems to the EQF and create National Qualifications Frameworks (NQF) in order to simplify comparisons across countries.

At the same time, the European Commission put forward an *Action Plan for Adult Learning "It is always a good time to learn" 2008-10*, which formulates five priorities for the adult learning sector: (1) analyse the effects of EQF, NQF and quality assurance systems reforms in all sectors of education and training in Member States on adult learning; (2) improve the quality of provisions in the adult learning sector, with a specific focus on the initial and continuing training of adult learning staff, quality standards and the accreditation of providers; (3) increase the possibilities for adults to go "one step up" and achieve a qualification at least one level higher than what they currently have; (4) speed up the process of assessment of skills and social competences and have them validated and recognised in terms of learning outcomes; and (5) improve the monitoring of adult learning sector, stressing the need for a common language, indicators and benchmarks, and comparable core data.

The 2010 *Bruges Communiqué* defined the priorities for the VET sector to 2020, prominently including the promotion of flexible pathways between the VET sector, general education, and higher education and the establishment of comprehensive national qualification frameworks based on learning outcomes (Dollhausen et al., 2013[8]). The *Communiqué* highlighted the creation of a *European Quality Assurance Reference Framework for Vocational Education and Training* (EQARF) and a *European Credit System for Vocational Education and Training* (ECVET) and setting deadlines for their implementation. ECVET allows learners to accumulate and transfer their learning in units, enabling learners to build a qualification at their own pace from learning outcomes acquired in both formal, non-formal and informal contexts. EQARF complements the work on quality assurance of the European Qualification Framework (EQF) and builds on the earlier Common Quality Assurance Framework (CQAF), providing a European-wide system to help countries monitor, evaluate and improve the effectiveness of their VET provision and quality management practices. The same year, the EQAVET network was established to replace the former ENQAVET platform, with the objective of encouraging and supporting the national implementation of the EQARF.

As a follow-up to the 2008-10 Action Plan, in 2011 the Council of the European Union approved a resolution on a renewed *European Agenda for Adult Learning* (2011/C 372/01) for the 2012-14 period. Among other recommendations, this document called for: raising motivation for participation; information and guidance systems; second-chance opportunities; flexible learning pathways; quality assurance systems and accreditation systems; and adult education staff training systems (Antunes, 2019[9]). As a consequence of these recommendations, a thematic working group (TWG) on quality in adult learning (comprising 19 Member States and 2 non-EU states) was established with the mandate of elaborating recommendations for the European Commission and the Member States on the development of quality assurance systems. Their final report came out at the end of 2013.

Finally, on 19 December 2016 the Council of the European Union adopted the Recommendation "*Upskilling Pathways: New Opportunities for Adults*", which made provision for a three-step mechanism focusing on skills assessment, provision of a tailored, flexible and quality learning offer, and validation and recognition of skills acquired. The Recommendation provides that, where possible, within one year of its adoption and at the latest by mid-2018, Member States should have outlined appropriate measures for the implementation at national level. Based on information provided by the Member States, the European Commission published in February 2019 a report taking stock of their implementation progress and showing that more efforts are required from Member States if they are to achieve the objectives of the Recommendation (European Commission, 2019[10]).

Table 1.1. Timeline of EU initiatives to improve quality of adult learning

Year	Initiative
2000	Lisbon Strategy 2000-10
2001	European Forum on Quality in VET
2002	Copenhagen Declaration
2004	CQAF
2005	ENQAVET
2008	EQF
2009	ECVET + EQARF + EQAVET
2010	Bruges Communiqué
2011	European Agenda for Adult Learning
2013	Quality in the Adult Learning Sector Report
2016	Recommendation on Upskilling Pathways

References

Antunes, F. (2019), "Europeanisation and adult education: between political centrality and fragility", *Studies in Continuing Education*, pp. 1-18, http://dx.doi.org/10.1080/0158037X.2019.1615425. [9]

Broek, S. and B. Buiskool (2013), *Developing the adult learning sector: Quality in the Adult Learning Sector*. [2]

Cedefop (2011), *Glossary: Quality in education and training*, Cedefop, Luxembourg, http://dx.doi.org/10.2801/94487. [1]

Dollhausen, K. et al. (2013), *Developing the adult learning sector - Opening higher education to adults*. [8]

European Commission (2019), *Council Recommendation on Upskilling Pathways: New Opportunities for Adults Taking stock of implementation measures*. [10]

European Commission (2013), *Thematic Working Group on Quality in Adult Learning Final Report*. [5]

Grossman, S. (1981), "An Introduction to the Theory of Rational Expectations Under Asymmetric Information", *The Review of Economic Studies*, Vol. 48/4, p. 541, http://dx.doi.org/10.2307/2297195. [7]

Hooley, T. and S. Rice (2019), "Ensuring quality in career guidance: a critical review", *British Journal of Guidance & Counselling*, Vol. 47/4, pp. 472-486, http://dx.doi.org/10.1080/03069885.2018.1480012. [6]

Latchem, C. (2012), *Quality Assurance Toolkit for Open and Distance Non-Formal Education*. [4]

OECD (2019), *Individual Learning Accounts : Panacea or Pandora's Box?*, OECD Publishing, Paris, https://dx.doi.org/10.1787/203b21a8-en. [11]

Prisăcariu, A. (2014), "Approaches of Quality Assurance Models on Adult Education Provisions", *Procedia - Social and Behavioral Sciences*, Vol. 142, pp. 133-139, http://dx.doi.org/10.1016/j.sbspro.2014.07.623. [3]

Notes

[1] While the terms "certification" and "accreditation" are often used interchangeably, they refer to two distinct processes (OECD, 2019[11]). Certifications guarantee that the necessary steps to achieve a certain level of compliance have been completed. Accreditation procedures, instead, are "the formal recognition by an appropriate authority that a body or a person is competent to carry out specific tasks" (Cedefop, 2011[1]), and they therefore guarantee that the bodies producing a certification are conform and competent to do so. Thus, accreditation and certification do not intervene at the same level: certification is delivered by certification bodies, while accreditation is delivered by accreditation bodies in charge to assess these certification bodies.

[2] Throughout the remainder of the report, the terms "certification" and "quality label" are used interchangeably.

2 Ensuring quality in adult learning through quality labels and certificates

Quality labels and certificates are typically part of the *regulatory approach* to quality development in adult learning as formal recognition by external bodies that training providers meet certain predetermined minimum quality requirements. They are used extensively throughout Europe with many successful experiences. Some of these quality labels exist since over 20 years, proving how effective they are in maintaining the quality of adult training. Although most certification processes follow similar practices, they remain very diverse in their implementation and in the quality criteria behind them.

Certifications and quality labels to ensure minimum quality levels

The eduQua certification framework in Switzerland

One of the best-known and long-standing certification frameworks in Europe is Switzerland's *eduQua*. At the turn of the millennium, the adult education sector in Switzerland was highly heterogeneous, with the market for adult learning dominated by many small private providers and no nation-wide regulation (in the Swiss federal system, responsibility for education lies with the 26 cantons). As a consequence, in 2000 the Swiss Federation for Adult Learning (SVEB) – an umbrella non-governmental organisation representing both public and private institutions, associations, and personnel managers – decided to introduce the quality label *eduQua*, with the support of the State Secretary for Economic Affairs, the cantons, and the Swiss Association of Employment Departments.

The main goal of the certification is to ensure that providers of adult learning meet some minimum standards at the time of registering (details on these minimum standards are presented later in this report). The certification process involves documentation but also on-site visits and yearly intermediate audits. All providers of adult education can apply for the certification, including those involved in the "re-skilling" of unemployed people. An important feature of the programme is that the *eduQua* label certifies the whole institution, and not its individual courses. Seven *eduQua* agencies conduct the certification, and over 1 000 Swiss adult learning providers are currently certified. The certification lasts three years, after which the provider must undergo a renewal. Each canton can choose whether providers need to have the *eduQua* certification to receive public funds, and at the moment this is the case in almost half of the cantons.

The involvement of the public sector in the creation and establishment of the label has been key not only in order to provide the necessary resources and funds in the initial phase, but also to ensure the involvement of all the different stakeholders. As a direct consequence of this, an Advisory Group was established at the outset, whose role is to identify quality criteria behind the label and decide on the requirements for the audits. The Group was originally chaired by the State Secretary and composed of an equal number of representatives from the state and from the different cantons as well as important players in the continuing education landscape (including public and private training providers from various sizes). The inclusive nature of the Advisory Group have proved crucial to ensure strong engagement of the different stakeholders in the initiative. Only after the label had been in place for 18 years and was mature enough to stand on its own feet, the State Secretary for Economic Affairs left the partnership.

The establishment of the *eduQua* quality label was also strongly supported by providers in an attempt to increase the perceived value of their training courses, and remain competitive vis-à-vis other education centres. This emerges clearly from the results of a survey conducted in 2017, where a majority of certified training institutions stated that they applied to the *eduQua* label because the whole procedure increases their recognition and credibility in the education market. The other two top motivations to apply for the certification flagged by respondents are also very important: providers see real improvements in the quality of their offer thanks to the certification process; and, in many cases, the label is a precondition for public funding.

With its two decades of experience, *eduQua* has proved to be very successful in signalling quality of training provision. Its main strengths lie in the fact that its scope is well defined, through a clear objective of certifying the quality of methodology and didactics in adult training only (rather than the whole education sector), and that it is managed by a well-respected main actor (Swiss Federation for Adult Learning, SVEB), which represents the interest of all stakeholders involved. The *eduQua* initiative itself had been regularly evaluated, allowing for incremental improvements that have increased its effectiveness over time. As a result, the label has received wide support from both policy makers, educational institutions and the private sector over the years.

The Greta-Plus, Eduform and Qualiopi labels in France

The *Greta-Plus* label in France provides some useful lessons on the importance of securing the buy-in of all relevant partners. The label was created in 2001 by the Ministry of Education with the aim of promoting the Greta (*groupement d'établissements publics locaux d'enseignement*, i.e. groups of public local providers of adult learning) in the face of private sector competition. The label emphasised the pedagogical dimension of training and the need to provide adults with tailor-made instruction whereby the learning paths and modalities are individualised. Whilst not compulsory, the government promoted the certification as a means of quality assurance. Yet, by 2013, more than a decade after the creation of the *Greta-Plus* label, only 43 of the 137 Greta had acquired the label (France Strategie, 2013[1]). This disappointing outcome was partly due a limited direct relevance to labour market needs. Indeed, according to Broek and Buiskool (2013[2]), local businesses – the most important "customers" of the Greta – saw little value in this label, thereby limiting Greta's incentives to apply for it. Moreover, it has also been argued that some Greta preferred not to request a *Greta-Plus* label in order to avoid the involvement of the central government in their functioning.

As a result, in 2017, the *Greta-Plus* label was discontinued and replaced by the new *Eduform* label. Also developed by the Ministry of Education, this new certification system promoting quality in the adult learning sector is applicable to both public and private adult training organisations. The *Eduform* label has the twofold purpose of boosting centres' attractiveness and quality by guaranteeing compliance with the AFNOR standards of continuous training services (AFNOR BP X50-762).[1] It is issued for three years after the completion of a national audit, although each year a follow-up audit is organised to review the attribution of the label. The National Council for Employment, Training and Vocational Guidance (CNEFOP) has included *Eduform* in the list of certificates and labels eligible for the Personal Training Account (CPF), meaning that prospective learners can use the balance on their Personal Training Account to take up courses in institutions with the *Eduform* label.

However, *Eduform* is not the only quality label available in France to certify providers of adult learning. In 2018, CNEFOP listed 32 recognised certificates.[2] Few of them are issued by public bodies (such as *Eduform* by the Ministry of Education or the *Certif'région* label by the Occitanie region), while the majority are produced by private entities (such as the *Cequaform* label by BCS Certification or *Qualiformapro* by Dekra Certification). Academic research suggests that, while not inherently problematic, the coexistence of multiple quality labels may lead to confusion among both providers, that are uncertain about which certificate to pursue, and prospective learners, who do not know which label to trust (Banerjee and Solomon, 2003[3]). Moreover, it might also lead to a race to the bottom, with providers applying for the most lenient certification among the ones available (Cashore, Auld and Newsom, 2003[4]).

In order to simplify this complex quality assurance landscape, in September 2018 the French Government passed a law establishing that all training centres that wish to obtain public funds must obtain a new quality certificate – *Qualiopi* – based on a single national quality reference system (*"Référentiel national de certification qualité des actions concourant au développement des compétences"* – RNCQ).[3] Providers can freely choose their certification body – as long as it is a body accredited by the French Accreditation Committee (COFRAC) – and must be certified by 1 January 2022 if they wish to receive public financing.[4] One of its peculiarities is that *Qualiopi* audits play a central role. In fact, not only do the certifying bodies carry out an on-site audit during the initial application process to ensure that what is self-reported by providers is properly implemented and corresponds to the RNCQ, but inspections take place one year later. If the certification body detects non-compliance, the label may be suspended or withdrawn. Moreover, when the *Qualiopi* label expires after three years, a new on-site audit is carried out to renew the certification for another three years.[5]

The certification of providers in Germany

The adult learning sector in Germany is less regulated by the state than other areas of education, under the assumption that local providers can more easily meet the diverse and rapidly changing demands of adult learners. Yet, over the years, there was a drive towards the certification of non-formal learning as an incentive for adults to engage more fully in society, leading to the elaboration of a nationwide certification process for all providers offering measures of active employment promotion in 2012. Under the process, providers have to be certified by specific bodies (*Fachkundige Stellen*) if they want to provide training. The German Accreditation Body (*Deutsche Akkreditierungsstelle*) is in charge of accrediting the certification bodies to make sure certification standards and procedures are adequate. The certification can be granted for a maximum of five years. If certified, providers can benefit from public funding.

Irrespective of the certifying body, the certification procedure for providers is structured in three stages. The first step involves the approval of the provider, and is mandatory for all; the prerequisites are efficiency and reliability, personnel and technical suitability, appropriate contractual conditions for the participants, and a quality assurance system (such as external quality management systems). In particular, this latter system for quality assurance must include requirements on: (i) customer orientation; (ii) continuous evaluation of training courses based on the use of indicators and measurement; (iii) continuous improvement of training provision; and (iv) cooperation with external experts for quality development. The second step involves the approval of the courses. For this, the certification body checks whether the course concept is likely to lead to successful completion, whether it is expedient, economical and whether it offers appropriate conditions for participation. The third stage is only necessary for providers of continuing vocational training and includes additional requirements for them.

The Initiative for Adult Education and the Ö-Cert quality label in Austria

In Austria, the adult education landscape is characterised by few national regulations and a large variety of stakeholders. No unified quality assurance system for non-formal adult learning exists, but a range of different instruments has been put in place over the past decade to ensure quality education. Two initiatives, in particular, have drawn great attention in the international debate on quality assurance: the Initiative for Adult Education and the label *Ö-Cert*.

The Initiative for Adult Education (*Initiative Erwachsenenbildung*) was established in 2012 by the Federal Ministry of Education together with the nine Austrian provinces, with the goal of creating high-quality courses enabling low-skilled adults to continue – and, in many cases, finish – their education. In addition to providing free courses for all participants, an important feature of the project is the implementation of consistent quality guidelines for all courses in the country. Accreditation is necessary for providers to take part in the initiative and it is based on three quality criteria: (1) fulfilment of general requirements; (2) creation of an appropriate programme concept; and (3) fulfilment of the project guidelines concerning the qualification of the trainers and counsellors. Once accredited, the provider can apply for public funding. Typically, for an approval to be granted, not only should the quality guidelines be met, but the programme should also fit with the needs of the participants in the region where it is conducted – in other words, funds are only granted when there is a need and a target group for the accredited offer. Providers taking part in the Initiative commit themselves to continuous monitoring and evaluation. This whole accreditation process is undertaken by six selected adult education experts, and a monitoring board supervises the process and the results.

In contrast, *Ö-Cert* is a quality framework ("umbrella label") for all adult education providers. Developed in 2011 by the Federal Ministry of Education and the nine Austrian provinces in cooperation with important stakeholders of adult education – such as the Conference of Adult Education Organizations – the aim of the label *Ö-Cert* was to reduce the administrative burdens that both providers, prospective learners and public authorities used to encounter in identifying quality training. In fact, depending on the definition used, there were between 1 800 and 3 000 providers in Austria in 2007, with offers that were often difficult to compare and little transparency for customers (Gruber, Brünner and Huss, 2009[5]). With rising attention on quality issues, providers had also gradually started to adopt a multitude of quality labels, systems and seals (e.g. ISO, EFQM, LQW, ...), making it so difficult for the government to assess their quality when applying for public funding that even provinces had started to create their own quality controls. The introduction of a single quality label was thus important not only to encourage homogeneity in quality assurance, but also to better manage the sector.

At its inception, Ö-Cert therefore had a challenging task: ensuring quality across educational institutions without being an additional quality management system. To address this, Ö-Cert not only committed to safeguard the principle of autonomy of providers, but – to not overburden all actors involved with a new quality management system – it pledged to be only a system of recognition and certification of quality without imposing their own audits. In practice, in order to be accredited with the Ö-Cert label, providers only need to have one of 11 Ö-Cert-approved Quality Management Systems or Quality Assurance Procedures. Hence, by using the concept of "umbrella label", this top-down procedure manages to respect the autonomy of decisions and use of different quality assurance systems by providers, while at the same time being an effective, simple and cheap model of introducing a transparent tool of quality in diverse contexts of the adult learning sector (Broek and Buiskool, 2013[2]). Since 2012, over 460 providers (1 266 including branches) have been accredited.

The NRTO and KET-KIT quality labels in the Netherlands

Similarly to Austria, in the Netherlands the adult education sector is also made up of numerous stakeholders and providers. While so far a nation-wide quality assurance system does not exist (but it is about to be created, see the last section of this chapter), in the past few years some quality initiatives have been put in place for a smaller subset of providers. For example, the Dutch Council for Education and Training (*Nederlandse Raad voor Training en Opleiding*, NRTO) is an umbrella trade association of about 300 private training and education providers, which established its own quality label. The *NRTO quality label* is based on an organisation's self-evaluation that is validated by an external auditor. The external audit is conducted by one of the three recognised organisations (*Kiwa Nederland, CPION, CIIO*) and costs around EUR 900. The basis of the *NRTO quality label* consists of eight quality requirements that are important for every private provider, from classroom trainers to providers of (online) training courses and exam and validation institutes. An NRTO member:

- Is transparent about its product or service;
- Is clear about the learning outcomes of education and training;
- Measures customer satisfaction;
- Fulfils agreements made;
- Uses knowledgeable teachers, trainers and advisors;
- Invests in the expertise of its staff;
- Has its processes in order;
- Strives for continuous improvement.

Like NRTO, three large language training organisations in the Netherlands – *ITTA, Radboud in'to Languages* and *VU NT2* – have established their own instrument to ensure quality in language education: KET-KIT (*Kwaliteitsinstrument Taalonderwijs van de Kwaliteitsgroep Educatie Taal*). KET-KIT distinguishes five quality areas (didactics, student guidance, facilities, management, and quality assurance) and within that a number of quality indicators and specific criteria, which have to be used to prepare a self-evaluation and which are then verified during an onsite inspection. If the self-evaluation and the audit provide evidence of sufficient quality, the organisation is given the *KET-KIT quality label* for two years. The standard price for KET-KIT is EUR 5 600.

The GKK quality framework in Belgium

In Flanders (Belgium), a distinction is made between adult education and adult training. On the one hand, adult education comprises all formal programmes of adult basic education, secondary adult education and adult higher vocational education. These courses are provided by the so-called Adult Education Centres and the Adult Basic Education Centres. On the other hand, adult training is a broader concept that includes, next to formal programmes, all forms of non-formal learning by adults, including the programmes offered by the Flemish Employment Services and Vocational Training Agency, socio-cultural organisations, private institutions, etc. While the Centres for Adult Basic Education and the Centres for Adult Education are required to implement a quality assurance system, until recently providers of non-formal training did not have a common quality assurance framework.

Only in June 2018 did the Flemish Government approve a preliminary draft by the Department of Education of a new common quality framework (*Gemeenschappelijk kwaliteitskader*, GKK) that aims at evaluating the quality of VET training provided by institutions outside the formal education system. The framework is based on the Flemish Qualification standards and is in line with the European Qualification Framework (OECD, 2019[6]). The proposal has been transformed into a decree in April 2019.[6] The new legislation states that non-formal or informal organisations that wish to offer recognised vocational programmes leading to a qualification that is part of the Flemish Qualification Structure must first apply for accreditation. As part of the process, a quality check is performed every six years, including on-site visits, by a neutral and independent external supervisory body. The framework includes the following quality areas:

- The objectives of the training correspond to the competences required by the relevant professional qualification;

- The design of the training is elaborated and organised in such a way that learners can acquire or demonstrate the competences required by the relevant professional qualification;

- The guidance of the learners implies that they are offered optimal opportunities to acquire or demonstrate the competences required by the relevant professional qualification;

- The evaluation of the learners allows to verify that they have acquired the competences required by the relevant professional qualification;

- the action points established in connection with the objectives, design, guidance and evaluation of the training lead to real quality improvements.

Box 2.1. Quality certificates outside Europe: The case of Korea and Chile

Training providers in Korea wishing to deliver government-funded training programmes need to be certified. The duration for which certification is granted depends on the outcome of the quality evaluation. The Korean Skills Quality Authority (KSQA) is in charge of the evaluation of vocational training providers, training programmes and trainees. The KSQA conducts an in-depth evaluation of institutions, including on financial soundness, capacity to provide training and training performance, and grants certified grades based on the evaluation outcomes. These grades are necessary to access government-funded training, and better performing institutions receive grades that are valid for longer periods (up to five years). The KSQA also screens training programmes in terms of content, methods, teacher quality, facilities and equipment, and past training outcomes. For the evaluation of the trainees, the KSQA assesses whether the participants who completed training courses have acquired the expected skills. Courses that have positive outcomes regarding trainee evaluation can receive additional financial support. The results from the trainee evaluation also feed into the training providers' evaluation.

In Chile, providers of training financed by the public employment services have to adhere to a Quality Norm that was set in 2015. Certification based on this Quality Norm is done by private entities (*Organismos certificadores de servicios*), which in turn are supervised by a public entity (*Instituto Nacional de Normas*). The aim of the Norm is to ensure that providers' management prioritise the satisfaction of the participants in the training activities and invest in the development of trainers' skills. The Norm also aims at periodically generate information on providers' financial results. When the Norm started to be enforced in 2017, this led to the closure of around 800 training providers. Complementary quality control mechanisms include ex-ante evaluations of training courses, evaluation of teaching staff (where studies, teaching and work experience of course trainers are evaluated), and on-site audit processes.

Source: OECD (2019[7]), Getting Skills Right: Future-Ready Adult Learning Systems, https://dx.doi.org/10.1787/9789264311756-en.

International quality standards

In addition to national certification frameworks, some international standards have also entered recently the market of quality assurance labels of adult learning. In particular, the most widely known are issued by the International Organization for Standardization (ISO). Founded in 1946, ISO is an independent, non-governmental international organisation with a membership of 164 national standards bodies (such as the American National Standards Institute – ANSI, France's ANFOR and the British Standards Institution – BSI).

In 2010, ISO created a new standard (*ISO 29990*) targeted specifically towards the design, development and delivery of non-formal education at all levels, including adult training. The standard focused on both providers' service provision and management systems. However, after recognising the growing complexity and diversity of the global market for learning services, the label was discontinued in 2017. To replace it, ISO created six new standards, each focusing on a particular aspect of quality in non-formal education. Depending on their objectives, contexts and external requirements (such as regulations or contractual arrangements), providers of non-formal training can now apply for a combination of these standards:

- *ISO 21001 "Management system for educational organisations"*

  This standard specifies management system requirements for a variety of educational organisations (both formal and non-formal). The standard draws on the following principles: (i) focus on learners and other beneficiaries; (ii) visionary leadership; (iii) engagement of people; (iv) process approach; (v) continual improvement; (vi) evidence-based decisions; (vii) relationship management; (viii) social responsibility; (ix) accessibility and equity; (x) ethical conduct; and (xi) data security and protection.

- *ISO 29991 "Language learning services outside formal education – Requirements"*

  This standard is aimed at organisations that provide language courses, solely or alongside other courses, outside formal education. It sets minimum requirements in terms of teaching staff, learning materials and environment, assessments, and advertising, among others. It will soon be replaced by the new – currently under development – standard ISO/DIS 29991.

- *ISO 29992 "Assessment of outcomes of learning services – Guidance"*

  This standard provides a framework for the development, implementation and use of results from assessments of learning outcomes. It provides guidance on the selection, validation, planning, administration and use of assessments in a range of learning outcomes.

- *ISO 29993 "Learning services outside formal education – Service requirements"*

    This standard specifies requirements for learning services outside formal education, including all types of lifelong learning (e.g. vocational training and in-company training, either outsourced or in-house). In particular, it aims at aligning various elements of learning services, including advertising, information provided to learners, needs analysis, design, assessment and evaluation, for the purpose of improving the effectiveness, efficiency and transparency of learning services.

- *ISO 29994 "Learning services outside formal education – Additional requirements for distance learning"*

    This standard is currently under development and not available yet.

- *ISO 29995 "Learning services outside formal education – Terminology"*

    This standard is currently under development and not available yet.

As all the standards developed by ISO are covered by copyright and patent laws, public access to their content in terms of minimum quality requirements is not available. For this reason, it is not possible to gauge the value of these standards and, therefore, are not considered further.

Common practices in certification processes

Although each quality assurance system has its own functioning, some practices are common to most certification processes. Indeed, four steps are regularly at the basis of certifications and quality label systems (Broek and Buiskool, 2013[2]). Firstly, providers of adult training must prepare their application dossier, filling up various forms and submitting a request to be quality assured. Frequently through self-evaluation reports, providers must assure that they comply with the standards requested by the certification organism. In a second step, the responsible body – be it a public, semi-public or private agency – carries out an external evaluation to assess the fulfilment of the required quality standards. This assessment can involve both on-site visits and inspections, expert consultations, and a validation of providers' self-reports. The third step is the approval of the application by the responsible body and the provision of the quality seal. Note that in many cases, the approval process by the certification organism is not merely "approved" or "not approved", but it involves scales of merit or conditional approval decisions.[7] The fourth and last common step in certification processes is the monitoring and follow-up of the approved quality seal. This may involve annual reports, on-site visits and – typically – the renewal of the label, if the certification was valid only for a limited time period.

For instance, in order to obtain the *Ö-Cert* label in Austria, candidate providers follow the steps outlined in Figure 2.1. First, the candidate institution needs to provide evidence of its identification as a provider of adult education, thereby fulfilling basic requirements concerning its organisation, offer and principles of ethics. In a second phase, the application is reviewed by the *Ö-Cert* Office.[8] In case there are documents missing or anything else is unclear, providers need to provide clarifications. In the third step, an accreditation group of experts[9] control using a checklist that the application of the provider is valid. The most important selection criterion here is the existence of external audits. This step therefore includes confirming that providers have one of the 11 valid quality management systems or quality assurance procedures included in the *Ö-Cert* list. If the request of accreditation is accepted, the provider is registered as one of the quality providers of adult education in Austria and receives the *Ö-Cert* label (after payment of an administration fee of EUR 100). As the *Ö-Cert* certification is only an umbrella label, its duration is the same as the duration of the quality management system that the providers have obtained (with a 6-month tolerance limit), although the validity period is not made available to the public.

Figure 2.1. Application process of *Ö-Cert*

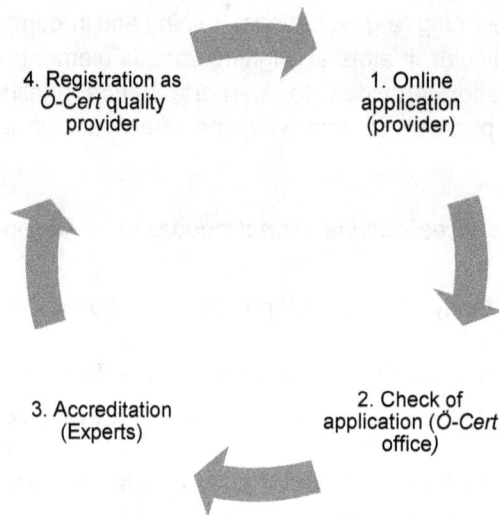

In a similar vein, providers of adult training applying for the *eduQua* label in Switzerland have to compile an application dossier following specific guidelines, where they need to prove their fulfilment of the minimum standards. The process differs from the Austrian initiative because there is an on-site audit, which has to be conducted before the evaluation of the dossier. The *eduQua* label is only awarded after the provider successfully passes the on-site audit and the dossier evaluation.

The *eduQua* label is also peculiar in its organisation, as pictured in Figure 2.2. In fact, the certification procedure is not performed by the *eduQua* office but by seven external certification bodies. These bodies are the ones evaluating in practice providers' fulfilment of the *eduQua* requirements, undertaking on-site audits, complaint handling, and helping providers meet the quality requirements. In order to become certification bodies of the *eduQua* label, organisations must be accredited by the Swiss Accreditation Service (SAS). Not only SAS assesses the competence of the certification bodies and their personnel for the correct performance of certifications (i.e. compliance with the rules of procedure), but it also ensures that the procedures of certification bodies remain satisfactory over time. Indeed, collusion between certification agencies and providers is a non-negligible risk, especially in a context where the former cannot compete on prices (certification fees are fixed by the *eduQua* Advisory Group). Relying on external bodies for the certification procedure allows *eduQua* to have only a small team of permanent people directly employed in their office, whose role is really to coordinate and ensure a smooth running of the organisational machine. This cuts *eduQua* office's running costs significantly, including also marketing expenses to publicise the *eduQua* label, since these expenses are paid directly by the certification bodies. As a result, the *eduQua* office manages to run by charging the certification bodies only roughly 10% of the overall certification fees paid by providers.

Figure 2.2. Organisation of the *eduQua* label

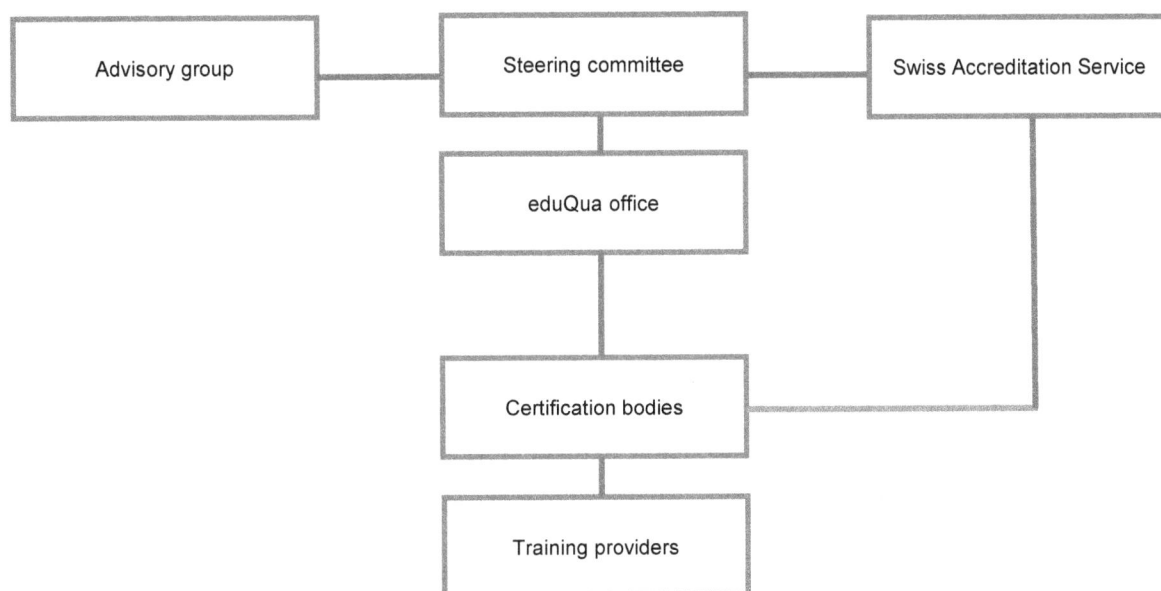

Source: Adapted from EduQua (2012[8]) *Manual eduQua: 2012: Information regarding the proceeding instruction for certification*, https://alice.ch/fileadmin/Dokumente/Qualitaet/eduQua/eduQua_Manual_2012_E.pdf.

Quality criteria used in certification processes

While, as shown above, most certification processes follow similar steps, identifying common quality standards used in the various certification systems is no easy task. In fact, detailed information about the specific criteria are often not publicly available, and – even when it is – quality standards vary considerably across contexts and quality assurance systems. Some focus more on accountability of the provider in terms of efficiency of how the public funds are spent, others concentrate on the quality of the didactics, and others instead prefer to focus on the quality of the learning outcomes.

Overall, four broad categories of quality criteria can be identified in certification processes (Broek and Buiskool, 2013[2]):

- First, quality standards on the organisational structure and management of the providers are almost ubiquitous in all certification processes across Europe. Typically, this set of criteria aims at ensuring that the provider has a well-defined and appropriate mission, its organisation is structured properly with solid management practices, the physical infrastructure of the provider is suitable for adult learning, and its finances are administered efficiently.

- Second, quality standards on the teaching staff of the providers are also frequently encompassed in most certification processes. Such type of standards includes setting minimum qualifications or competence levels and offering further training for the adult trainers themselves.

- Third, quality of didactics and the learning process, although not all certification processes stress this aspect equally. The goal of these specific standards is to make sure the educational offer of the provider fits with the needs of adult learners. This third category of quality criteria includes for example guidance and counselling for learners, complaint procedures, assessments of the quality of exams and evaluations, education and training methods, etc.

- Fourth, quality of training outcomes, which is included in most certification processes to evaluate providers. Relevant criteria include follow-up evaluations of training programmes, feedback from students, labour market performance of past learners, etc.

The case of the *eduQua* label in Switzerland illustrates well the sort of quality standards that certification processes use in practice to evaluate adult education providers. To measure the quality of a provider, *eduQua* uses 22 well-defined standards grouped in six criteria, which are all listed in a publicly available manual (EduQua, 2012[8]). For each of the 22 standards, the manual precisely defines:

- The objectives of the standard and why it has been selected;
- The requirements to respect;
- The indicators that can be used to evaluate the standard;
- The documents that the provider needs to send to the *eduQua* agency during the certification process; and
- The documents that will be needed when the certification agency will perform an on-site audit at the provider's premises.

The list of 6 criteria and 22 standards is presented in Table 2.1, while Box 2.2 shows an example of how detailed is the discussion of criteria and standards in the *eduQua* manual.

It is interesting to note how the *eduQua* quality criteria have already been subject to three revisions since the creation of the label, with a new revision planned for 2021, in order to improve and meet the fast-changing nature of the adult education landscape. Among the latest changes, one that seems particularly important is the move away from more standardised, rigid teaching/learning processes to the facilitation of individual, independent learning pathways – in line with the latest recommendations from the European Union.

Table 2.1. The quality criteria behind the *eduQua* label in Switzerland

Criterion	Standards
Training offers that satisfy the needs of the customer and society at large	1. Definition of courses 2. Learning objectives 3. Learning content 4. Verification of the achieved learning success 5. Evaluation of courses
A transparent presentation of continuing education opportunities, the institution and its guidelines	6. Information about the provider 7. Information about the courses
A training that allows, facilitates and promotes the success of learning	8. Selection of participants 9. Lesson planning 10. Teaching and learning methods 11. Teaching instruments and media 12. Transfer of learning
Qualified trainers, with high skills in methodology and didactics as well as in their specialisation	13. Qualifications 14. Activities of continuing education and development 15. Feedback for trainers
Conventions and commitments that are reviewed and respected; continuous development of quality that is ensured	16. Quality assurance and quality development
A management that guarantees customer-oriented, economical, efficient and effective services	17. Institutional mission statement and andragogic guiding principles 18. Management instruments 19. Organisation 20. Classrooms and infrastructure 21. Customer satisfaction 22. Monitoring and further development

Source: EduQua (2012[8]), *Manual eduQua: 2012: Information regarding the proceeding instruction for certification*, https://alice.ch/fileadmin/Dokumente/Qualitaet/eduQua/eduQua_Manual_2012_E.pdf.

> ### Box 2.2. The importance of details: evidence from *eduQua* certification manual
>
> The level of granularity that the *eduQua* manual provides for each standard can be illustrated taking one particular standard as an example. For instance, standard 21 "Customer satisfaction" has been chosen in order to provide comprehensive and good quality customer services. Participant satisfaction should not be limited to aspects of training, but also take into account other important features of the institution, such as its infrastructure and its websites. The requirements for this standard include, among others, the presence of regular customer surveys and an efficient complaint service. The indicators used to evaluate this standard refer to the correct implementation of improvement measures following the evaluation of customers' satisfaction.
>
> The documents that the provider needs to include in its application package should contain information on the measurement, evaluation and development of customer satisfaction over the previous three years, also specifying the exact instruments and methods used. When the *eduQua* agency carries out the on-site audit, it checks not only the result of the assessment of customer satisfaction, but also the improvement measures implemented. Moreover, the manual also provides additional questions and themes that may be discussed during the on-site visit, such as the main additional benefits for participants (e.g. free parking near the institution, cafeteria, etc.) and how these can be taken into account in the customer satisfaction evaluation.
>
> As shown, the level of details for each criteria used in the *eduQua* certification process is very high, and it is important to acknowledge the effort put by the decision makers behind the *eduQua* label in providing such clear and transparent evaluation guidelines. This level of details is particularly important in the Swiss context to ensure that the different certification agencies use the same standards to evaluate providers.
>
> Source: EduQua (2012[8]), *Manual eduQua: 2012: Information regarding the proceeding instruction for certification*, https://alice.ch/fileadmin/Dokumente/Qualitaet/eduQua/eduQua_Manual_2012_E.pdf.

The basic requirements for acceptance into the quality framework for adult education *Ö-Cert* in Austria are slightly less detailed yet still clearly defined. The provider has to fulfil five categories of basic requirements: general basic requirements, basic requirements concerning the organisation of the provider, basic requirements concerning the offers of the provider, basic requirements concerning principles of ethics and democracy, and basic requirements with regard to quality (Table 2.2). Providers need to submit a mission statement, an organisation chart, terms of business, proofs from a person with pedagogical knowledge, the course program and a valid quality certificate.

Table 2.2. The quality criteria behind the *Ö-Cert* label in Austria

Criterion	Standards
General basic requirements, central paradigms of the adult education provider	• Basic philosophy of education – Education has its own value in any stages of life: It affects political involvement, social life, professional efficiency and personal identity in a positive way. Education can be considered more than instrumental learning qualifications and further training. • Lifelong learning – Lifelong learning embraces all formal, non-formal and informal acquisition of knowledge in various educational centres reaching from childhood up to the stage of retirement. Lifelong learning can be defined as any act of learning with a definite goal, which serves the purpose of continuous improvement of knowledge, abilities and competences. Here "learning" is viewed as a processing of information and experiences into knowledge, insight and competences. Verification of the achieved learning success • Adult education/Continuing education and training – Adult education (synonymous with continuing education and training) includes all forms of formal, non-formal and informal goal-orientated learning by adults after completion of a first stage of education varying in length and irrespective of the level that has been reached during this process. Adult education/Continuing education and training involves all vocational, political and

Criterion	Standards
	cultural teaching and learning processes or those, which offer basic education for adults and are controlled within a public, private and economic context by others or oneself. Adult education-orientated action is based on political strategies in education, social responsibility, organisational structures as well as legal and financial requirements. • Definition of providers – Any type of organisation (associations, businesses, institutes, coordinating organisations of networks and cooperation), which offers adult education/continuing education and training according to the definitions set out above, can be termed providers.
Basic requirements with regard to organisation	• The organisation requires at least one educational offer in Austria, which is characterised by regularity, plans and systematisation and must be communicated in public; transparency of provision is prevalent. • Adult education/ Continuing education and training is the core task of the organisation. • At the time of application the organisation is required to have provided measures in adult education/continuing education and training for at least 3 economic or calendar years. • The head of the organisation or at least one employee must have undertaken thorough pedagogical education or further training and have appropriate work experience of two years. • Terms of business of the organisation need to be publicly transparent and made available to the public.
Basic requirements with regard to provision	• In general, the organisation's provision of education is made available publicly or if the need arises is aimed at target groups (such as women, the elderly, migrants, trainings for librarians, trade unions). • Offers of formal education at schools and universities are accepted, if they are aimed at adults with the purpose of gaining further qualifications within the framework of continuing education and training. Undergraduate courses of study at public and private universities, universities for applied science and pedagogical universities do not fall into this category. • Organisations with their offers feel under an obligation to the set out democratic values of the responsible bodies and sponsors of Ö-Cert (federal states and federal government). • The public libraries are key representatives in adult education/ continuing education and training. In accordance with Ö-Cert only organisations which provide offers (such as courses, readings) with a focus on active impartation of knowledge are acknowledged. • Organisations, which primarily offer trainings with a focus on particular products and/or events, which are primarily tailored to customers and attract new members, are excluded by Ö-Cert. Trainings in the field of users' programmes such as Microsoft Office do not fall into the category "trainings" with a focus on particular products". • Organisations, which provide individual guidance and counselling in the field of education and training as an applied method within the framework of an educational process, are acknowledged in accordance with Ö-Cert. Organisations, whose offers are exclusively aimed at individuals on a one-to-one basis, are not taken into consideration. • Organisations, which primarily provide activities that solely encourage the individual to engage in sports and exercise and offer leisure time activities, are not taken into consideration in accordance with Ö-Cert. • Organisations, which provide cultural offers, are taken into consideration in accordance with Ö-Cert, if the events serve the purpose of imparting cultural knowledge. Performances of any kind and exhibitions are not included. • In a religious, ideological context the organisation's intent of impartation must exceed the practical application in accordance with Ö-Cert, such as events, where propagation of faith is prevalent, are not taken into consideration.
Basic requirements with regard to ethical and democratic principles	• The organisation acknowledges the current Universal Declaration of Human Rights. This ensures that all persons irrespective of their gender and age, their education, their social and professional status, their political and ideological beliefs and their nationality have access to education. During the educational process, freedom of speech is guaranteed and encouraged. • The organisation is under an obligation to democracy. According to this self-explanatory term no antidemocratic, racist, anti-Semitic and sexist materials and behaviours are accepted, neither are such materials and behaviours, which discriminate against other individuals. These materials, tendencies and behaviours are counteracted in the educational sessions. In addition the organisation does not provide any space for the propaganda of antidemocratic ideologies, it does not offer any possibility for other forms of propaganda, agitation or advertisement of products or the recruitment of "clientele" for political, religious and other ideological groups.
Basic requirements with regard to quality	• The organisation must hold an external certificate of quality, which has been approved of by Ö-Cert.[1]

1. The 11 valid external certificates of quality are: ISO 9001: 2008, ISO 29990: 2010, EFQM, LQW (Learner-Oriented Quality Certification for Further Education Organizations/Germany), QVB (Quality development in the array of educational institutions/Germany), EduQua (the Swiss quality label), UZB (environment-label/Ministry of Agriculture), four quality management systems of Austrian federal states: Salzburg, Vienna, Upper Austria, Lower Austria. The main common feature of these different certifications is that they all have an external audit.

Source: Ö-Cert (2019[9]), *Ö-CERT [AT-Cert]: An overall framework of quality for Adult Education in Austria*, https://oe-cert.at/media/OE-Cert_abstract.pdf.

In a similar vein, the recent French *Qualiopi* certification is based on the new national quality reference system ("*Référentiel national de certification qualité des actions concourant au développement des compétences*" – RNCQ), which is also very detailed. The RNCQ is organised around seven criteria linked to 22 indicators which apply to all providers (common core), to which 10 other indicators are added specifically for apprenticeship and training leading to a certification (Table 2.3).[10] Box 2.3 presents another example of quality criteria used for a quality certification of career guidance services rather than for adult learning.

Table 2.3. The quality criteria behind the *Qualiopi* label in France

Criterion	Standards
The conditions for informing the public about the services offered, the deadlines for accessing them and the results obtained	1. The service provider disseminates detailed and verifiable information accessible to the public on the services offered: prerequisites, objectives, duration, terms and access times, prices, contacts, methods used and evaluation methods, accessibility for disabled people. 2. The service provider disseminates result indicators adapted to the nature of the services provided and audiences welcomed. 3. When the service provider implements services leading to professional certification, it informs about the rates of obtaining prepared certifications, the possibilities to validate one / or blocks of skills, as well as equivalences, *passerelles*, and future opportunities.
The precise identification of the objectives of the services offered and the adaptation of these services to the beneficiary audience when designing them	4. The service provider analyses the beneficiary's need in relation to the company and / or the funding body concerned. 5. The service provider defines the operational and assessable objectives of the service. 6. The service provider establishes the content and the methods of implementing the service, adapted to the defined objectives and the beneficiary audiences. 7. When the service provider implements services leading to certification professional, he ensures the adequacy of the content or content of the service to the requirements of the certification concerned. 8. The service provider determines the positioning and assessment procedures at the entrance to the service.
Adaptation to the audiences benefiting from the services and methods of reception, support, monitoring and evaluation implemented	9. The service provider informs the beneficiary audiences of the conditions of the service. 10. The service provider implements and adapts the service, support and monitoring to beneficiary audiences. 11. The service provider assesses the achievement by the beneficiaries of the service objectives. 12. The service provider describes and implements the measures to encourage engagement of beneficiaries and prevent breaks in the route. 13. For work-linked training, the service provider, in connection with the company, anticipates with the learner the missions entrusted, in the short, medium and long term, and ensures coordination and the progressiveness of the learning carried out in the training centre and in the company. 14. The provider implements socio-professional, educational support and relating to the exercise of citizenship. 15. The service provider informs apprentices of their rights and duties as apprentices and employees as well as applicable health and safety rules in the workplace professional. 16. When the service provider implements training courses leading to certification professional, it ensures that the conditions of presentation of beneficiaries for certification meet the formal requirements of the certification authority.
The adequacy of teaching, technical and supervisory resources to the services implemented	17. The service provider makes available or ensures the provision of the means human and technical resources and an appropriate environment (conditions, premises, equipment, technical platforms, etc.). 18. The service provider mobilises and coordinates the various internal stakeholders and / or external (educational, administrative, logistical, commercial, etc.). 19. The service provider provides the beneficiary with educational resources and allows it is up to him to appropriate them. 20. The service provider has staff dedicated to supporting national and international mobility, a disability adviser and professional development advice.
The qualification and development of knowledge and skills of the staff	21. The service provider determines, mobilises and assesses the skills of the various internal and / or external stakeholders, adapted to the services. 22. The service provider maintains and develops the skills of its employees, adapted to the benefits it delivers.

Criterion	Standards
The provider's investment in its professional environment	23. The service provider carries out a legal and regulatory watch on the field of training and learns from it.
	24. The service provider monitors trends in skills and trades and jobs in its areas of intervention and learning from it.
	25. The service provider monitors educational and technological innovations allowing an evolution of its services and exploiting the lessons learned.
	26. The service provider mobilises the expertise, tools and networks necessary to host, support / train or guide people with disabilities.
	27. When the service provider uses subcontracting or wage portage, he ensures compliance with this standard.
	28. When the services provided to the beneficiary include periods of training in the workplace, the service provider mobilises its network of partners socio-economic to co-build training engineering and foster welcoming business.
	29. The provider develops actions that contribute to professional integration or the pursuit of study by the way of the apprenticeship or by any other way allowing to develop their knowledge and skills.
Collecting and taking into account assessments and complaints	30. The service provider receives feedback from stakeholders: beneficiaries, financiers, teaching teams and companies involved.
	31. The service provider implements methods for dealing with difficulties encountered by stakeholders, complaints made by them, uncertainties occurred during service.
	32. The service provider implements improvement measures based on the analysis of appreciations and complaints.

Source: French Ministry of Labour (2020[10]), *Référetiel National Qualité mentionné à l'article L. 6316-3 du Code du Travail*, https://travail-emploi.gouv.fr/IMG/pdf/guide_referentiel_qualite_28-02.pdf.

Box 2.3. Criteria used for quality certification of career guidance services: the case of the Matrix Standard in the United Kingdom

Launched in 2002 by the British Department for Education, the *Matrix Standard* is a quality certification assigned to organisations that deliver information, advice and/or guidance (IAG) services, either as their sole activity or as part of their wider offering. It aims at supporting individuals in their choice of career, learning, work and life goals by ensuring that IAG providers meet a certain level of competency. It helps providers improve their services by benchmarking against best practices and it offers certification to those that meet the full standard. Organisations that can apply to the certificate include training providers, universities, voluntary and community organisations, and private businesses. While the Standard is typically voluntary, it becomes a prerequisite to access public funding in particular cases.

The *Matrix Standard* is outcome-based, which means it does not focus only on processes used to support IAG delivery but also looks at results achieved. Overall, an organisation needs to prove that: (i) they know and clearly define what they offer to their learners; (ii) they provide accurate, impartial, up-to-date information; (iii) they allow learners to make informed decisions; and (iv) they continuously evaluate and improve the training and information provided. In particular, the 27 quality criteria that Further Education Establishments need to meet are grouped into the following headings:[1]

- *Leadership and management*: the services provided have precise objectives and clear leadership; the organisation complies with existing legislation, operates with integrity and cooperates with other bodies; clients' outcomes are at the centre of the services, and their outcomes measure the success of the service.

- *Resources*: the organisation uses its resources effectively; clients are provided with accurate information; staff has the appropriate qualification and are supported in continuous professional development.

- *Service delivery*: the services provided are impartial and effective to meet predetermined objectives; clients are responsible for making their own decisions and, when exploring options, are supported with appropriate resources, including and referral to other appropriate organisations.

- *Continuous quality improvement*: the organisation evaluates its services against its objectives and identifies improvements; both customers' satisfaction and staff performance are also evaluated; effective use is made of technology to improve the service; the quality assurance process is continuous and dynamic.

1. The complete manual with the quality criteria, instructions for assessments and example are available at: https://matrixstandard.com/media/1058/the-matrix-standard-guidance-for-fe-establishments-20190107.pdf.

Yet, not all certification initiatives need to have such level of details and granularity in terms of their quality requirements. Less complex quality assurance mechanisms may also have some advantages. For instance, there is evidence that consumers often react more to information that are easier to understand than to more sophisticated – but perhaps more objective – quality systems (Dafny and Dranove, 2008[11]). An example of more straightforward quality labels is the *label de qualité* created in 2000 for the non-formal adult education sector in Luxembourg. The aim of the label is twofold: improving providers' quality, as well as supporting the monitoring of the otherwise difficult-to-regulate non-formal sector, allowing the government to gather data and information. The requirements that providers of adult training need to meet in order to obtain the *label de qualité* of Luxembourg are only ten, and they refer mostly to organisational aspects of the training (e.g. minimum number of participants in each course and special fees for disadvantages groups) or staff qualifications. Similarly, the *Eduform* label in France is based on a high level of requirements for 13 commitments, as well as for the organisation and management of the targeted structures (Box 2.4).

Box 2.4. The requirements of more slender quality labels: the Luxembourg and French experiences

The requirements of the *label de qualité* in Luxembourg

1. A minimum of 15 learners (exceptions are possible for certain courses);
2. Guaranteeing general access to the courses;
3. Availability of a special enrolment rate (EUR 5 to 10) to disadvantaged target groups;
4. Publishing the courses including information on learning outcomes;
5. Advising the learners to find the right offer;
6. Providing information about accessibility for persons with special needs;
7. Applying a pedagogical approach based on the needs and the situation of adults;
8. Teachers must be accredited by the Minister (pedagogical and content-related competences achieved either through initial education, continuous education or professional experience);
9. Delivering a participation certificate to learners who attend 70% of the course;
10. Delivering on demand an individual certificate including the description of skills and knowledge obtained.

The commitments of the *Eduform* label in France

1. Quick and guided access to information on the services offered;
2. Quality of the reception;
3. Personalised advice on the services and their financing possibilities;
4. Proposal of a wide range of services;
5. Help in building a tailor-made response;
6. Contractualisation with the beneficiary on the objectives, the contents and the modalities of the services;
7. Support, monitoring, evaluation and readjustment of the beneficiary's journey throughout the service by a dedicated person;
8. Adaptation to each service and for each beneficiary of the premises and the pedagogical means, methods, supports, tools and materials of the service;
9. Assessment and recognition of prior learning and certification;
10. Qualifications and competencies guaranteed and developed throughout life;
11. Taking into account the satisfaction of customers and beneficiaries;
12. Continuous improvement of services and trainings;
13. Taking into account stakeholder expectations of corporate social responsibility and sustainable development.

References

Banerjee, A. and B. Solomon (2003), "Eco-labeling for energy efficiency and sustainability: A meta-evaluation of US programs", *Energy Policy*, Vol. 31/2, pp. 109-123, http://dx.doi.org/10.1016/S0301-4215(02)00012-5. [3]

Broek, S. and B. Buiskool (2013), *Developing the adult learning sector: Quality in the Adult Learning Sector*. [2]

Cashore, B., G. Auld and D. Newsom (2003), "Forest certification (eco-labeling) programs and their policy-making authority: Explaining divergence among North American and European case studies", *Forest Policy and Economics*, Vol. 5/3, pp. 225-247, http://dx.doi.org/10.1016/S1389-9341(02)00060-6. [4]

Dafny, L. and D. Dranove (2008), "Do report cards tell consumers anything they don't already know? The case of Medicare HMOs", *RAND Journal of Economics*, Vol. 39/3, pp. 790-821, http://dx.doi.org/10.1111/j.1756-2171.2008.00039.x. [11]

EduQua (2012), *Manual eduQua: 2012: Information regarding the proceeding instruction for certification*, https://alice.ch/fileadmin/Dokumente/Qualitaet/eduQua/eduQua_Manual_2012_E.pdf. [8]

France Strategie (2013), *Le marché de la formation professionnelle continue à l'épreuve de l'enjeu de la qualité*. [1]

French Ministry of Labour (2020), *Référetiel National Qualité mentionné à l'article L. 6316-3 du Code du Travail*, https://travail-emploi.gouv.fr/IMG/pdf/guide_referentiel_qualite_28-02.pdf. [10]

Gruber, A., S. Brünner and E. Huss (2009), *Perspektiven der Erwachsenenbildung im Rahmen des lebenslangen Lernens in der Steiermark (PERLS)*. [5]

Ö-Cert (2019), *Ö-CERT [AT-Cert] - an overall framework of quality for Adult Education in Austria*, https://oe-cert.at/media/OE-Cert_abstract.pdf. [9]

OECD (2019), *Getting Skills Right: Future-Ready Adult Learning Systems*, Getting Skills Right, OECD Publishing, Paris, https://dx.doi.org/10.1787/9789264311756-en. [7]

OECD (2019), *OECD Skills Strategy Flanders: Assessment and Recommendations*, OECD Skills Studies, OECD Publishing, Paris, https://dx.doi.org/10.1787/9789264309791-en. [6]

Notes

[1] ANFOR is the French Standardisation Association (*Association Française de Normalisation*), which is in charge of developing international standardisation activities, information provision and certification in France. Its standard BP X50-762 proposes criteria of quality for the services offered by providers of continuing professional training. It specifies, in the organisational provisions, their conditions of implementation and mentions how the management intends to define, promote, monitor and improve its policy in terms of quality of service.

[2] http://www.cnefop.gouv.fr/qualite/liste-des-certifications-et-labels-generalistes-du-cnefop.html.

[3] Without this new certification, organisations can only work as training provider for companies managing their own skills development plans.

[4] While initially set to 1 January 2021, the date by which all providers need to have the new certification has been postponed by a year, due to the COVID-19 crisis.

[5] The training organisation can at this stage change certification body.

[6] The decree text can be found here: https://data-onderwijs.vlaanderen.be/edulex/document.aspx?docid=15324.

[7] For example, in Switzerland the *eduQua* label can be granted unconditionally or conditionally under certain conditions that are clearly stipulated. Similarly, in France the committee in charge of assigning the *Eduform* label has four options: a) grant the label for 3 years; b) deny the label; c) demand additional information; and d) demand another audit.

[8] Only four people work in the *Ö-Cert* Office. Their role is to make the first check of the applications and be responsible for the central organisation of the label.

[9] The accreditation group is a group of five experts who are responsible for the accreditation of providers; they assess the proofs and meet approximately 5-7 times a year.

[10] The full manual (in French) is available here: https://travail-emploi.gouv.fr/IMG/pdf/guide_referentiel_qualite_28-02.pdf.

3 Ensuring quality in adult learning through evaluations

Evaluations are an important tool of quality assurance in adult learning. In particular, the practice of self-evaluations has been widely adopted throughout Europe, especially in non-formal training, since it allows providers to assess their own quality and implement plans to improve it over time that fit with their needs and constraints. Evaluations undertaken by external bodies are also common and valued because of their hybrid nature: they resemble self-evaluations in their functioning, but they are similar to quality certificates in their typically mandatory approach. In both cases, the production of guidelines and other support materials by public authorities has proved very effective to facilitate providers' own evaluations.

Self-evaluations to foster a quality culture

In Slovenia, self-evaluation is commonly used among education and training providers and was until recently part of an *advisory approach* to quality assurance. This practice is now very much rooted in the sector partly thanks to a quality framework applying to adult learning that was introduced in 2001 for explicit use for self-evaluation by entire institutions or specific programmes. Moreover, the Slovenian Institute of Adult Education launched the Offering Quality Education to Adults (OQEA) initiative in 1999 to advise educational organisations on how to self-evaluate their own quality and determine their future development. The OQEA approach to self-evaluation is based on the principles of definition, assessment, maintenance and development of quality of one's own work. During this process, the management and the employees reflect on their own mission, vision and values they want to develop through their education of adults. The approach includes tools for planning and implementation of continuous monitoring and in-depth assessment of the quality of services and planning of measures for constant improvement to ensure the satisfaction of organisations, of the adult learner and of business partners and the environment.

The Slovenian Institute of Adult Education also started a systematic collection of areas and indicators of quality in adult education that organisations can use in self-evaluation. There are almost 100 indicators and criteria to choose from, which are grouped into 11 overarching quality areas (Slovenian Institute of Adult Education, 2013[1]). These latter quality areas are structured depending on whether they represent: (i) transverse factors of quality, (ii) input – or infrastructural – factors, (iii) process factors, or (iv) output factors (Figure 3.1). Transverse factors include activities and processes that cannot simply be placed among the input, process or output factors, but they touch all of them. This is particularly the case of management and administration, which define the quality of the management processes from organisational and contents point of view, on different levels, in different processes. Input factors are the production factors that must be ensured before the education even begins, and consist of educational programmes, promotion of adult education, stimulating adults to enter education, staff, premises and equipment. Among the process factors a key role is played by the planning of education and the implementation of education. In addition, the development work to support the education process and the support of individuals in education are also central. They in fact complement the previous two fields, given that, in adult education, support to individuals is almost as important as the education itself, and without development work it is difficult to imagine any kind of progress, particularly progress in quality development. Finally, output quality factors are those seen as the results and effects of education activities.

Figure 3.1. Quality areas by the Slovenian Institute of Adult Education

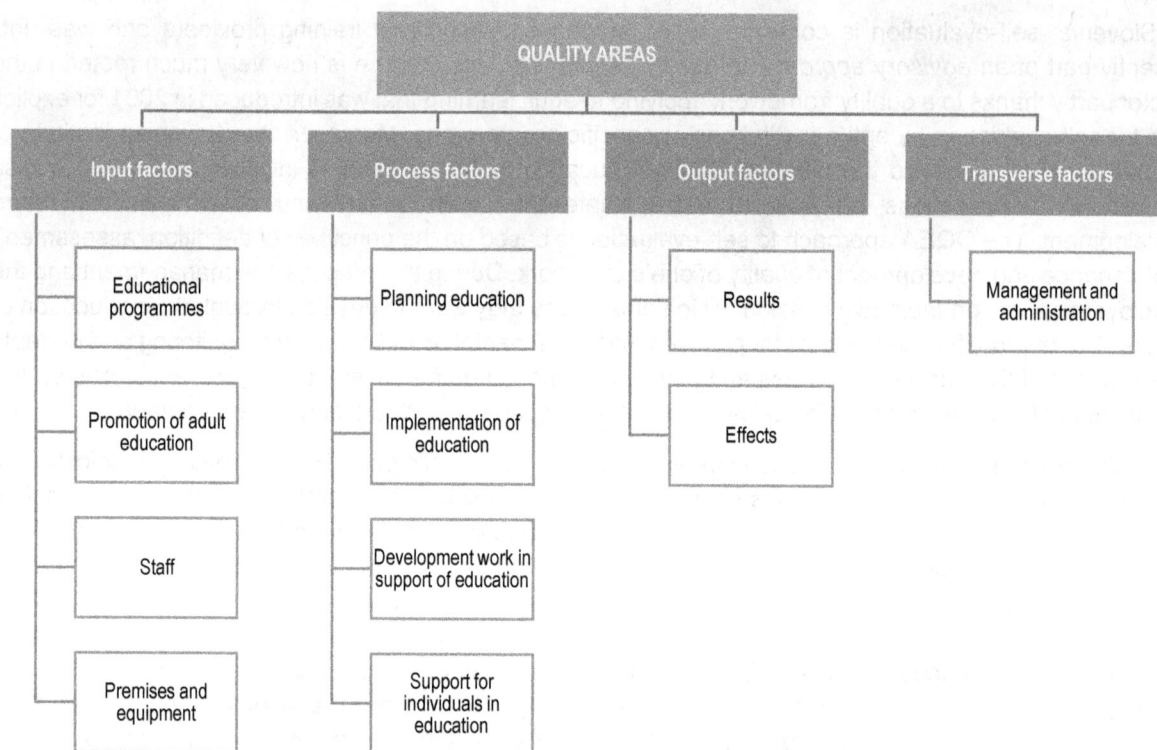

```
                           ┌──────────────────┐
                           │  QUALITY AREAS   │
                           └──────────────────┘
        ┌──────────────┬──────────────┬──────────────┐
┌───────────────┐ ┌───────────────┐ ┌───────────────┐ ┌───────────────────┐
│ Input factors │ │Process factors│ │ Output factors│ │Transverse factors │
└───────────────┘ └───────────────┘ └───────────────┘ └───────────────────┘
```

Input factors	Process factors	Output factors	Transverse factors
Educational programmes	Planning education	Results	Management and administration
Promotion of adult education	Implementation of education	Effects	
Staff	Development work in support of education		
Premises and equipment	Support for individuals in education		

Source: Adapted from Slovenian Institute of Adult Education (2013[1]), *Quality indicators in adult education.*

OQEA has a logo that all providers of adult education can obtain if they prove that in the past three years they have carried out self-evaluation processes systematically and produced a written action plan based on the derived in-depth self-evaluation. Note that, in contrast to the quality labels described in the previous section, the purpose of the OQEA quality logo is not to certify the fulfilment of minimum binding quality requirements. Rather, the logo aims at rewarding adult training providers who care about how they do their work and are prepared to constantly learn, test new findings, systematically assess the effects of their work and implement measures to develop quality (Broek and Buiskool, 2013[2]). Currently, approximately 40 providers have obtained the OEQA logo.[1]

Building on this two-decade experience of encouraging a quality culture through self-evaluation, the Slovenian Government adopted the Adult Education Act in 2018, which effectively switched Slovenia's approach to quality assurance in adult education from *advisory* to *regulatory* while still using self-evaluation as a tool. In fact, the 2018 Adult Education Act requires all adult education providers to have an internal quality system that includes ongoing monitoring and in-depth self-evaluation. Information on how providers conduct their self-evaluations also have to be made available publicly.

The case of Hungary is similar. In fact, Hungary recently adopted two legislative piece – Act LXXVII of 2013 and Decree 11/2020 – which in practice establish a *regulatory approach* to quality assurance based purely on self-evaluation. According to the more recent legislation, providers of adult learning need to have a quality management system based on self-evaluation to operate. Although the government has set certain overarching elements that providers should tackle with their quality assurance systems, the responsibility of identifying the correct quality indicators and general framework is left completely to the institutions themselves. No training on how to develop a quality management system and conduct self-evaluation is provided.

Recent efforts in Portugal also attempt to encourage the creation of a self-evaluation culture among the *Qualifica Centres*, which provide guidance and support for recognition of prior learning. In particular, the Centres have to submit information on enrolment, referral to education and training pathways and recognition activities to the National Agency for Qualification and Vocational Education (ANQEP), which analyses the information and sends it back to the centres in an effort to encourage self-evaluation. Self-evaluations are also common in the formal adult education sector: Box 3.1 presents, for example, the case of the well-known BRUK system in Sweden.

A more subjective way to measure quality is the satisfaction of participants with the training they undertake. This is generally measured through surveys during and/or after training participation. In the Brussels capital region (Belgium), the results from user satisfaction surveys are part of the quality evaluation done by *Bruxelles Formation*, the organisation in charge of adult learning for the French-speaking population in Brussels. They aim to have an average satisfaction level of at least eight out of ten, on a scale from 1 to 10 where 1 is the lowest satisfaction level. In Finland, participants' surveys are run during and right after every training programme funded by the public employment services, and this information feeds into the evaluation process.

Box 3.1. Self-evaluation in formal adult education: The case of BRUK in Sweden

The *Bedömning, Reflektion, Utveckling, Kvalitet* (Assessment, Reflection, Development, Quality) initiative (BRUK) is a general support system developed by school authorities in Sweden in 2001 for quality assurance in preschools and public schools, and adapted specifically to formal adult education in 2008. It is based on a set of self-evaluation tools and indicators, as elaborated in national steering documents. By showing strengths and weaknesses of adult training providers, the BRUK quality model aims at giving an overview of the overall quality of the institutions and areas for improvement.

Fundamentally, the system is based on a list of questions that providers of adult training ask themselves with the final goal of identifying gaps in the quality of the delivery of their services. The structure of the questions is complex, yet elaborated such that it maximise continuous improvement. Three main areas – process, goal achievement, and contextual factors – are split into a number of indicator areas, which are then divided in sub-areas and in numerous sub-indicators. For each of these indicators and sub-indicators, precise criteria are then enumerated, and providers need to assess to what extent such criteria are met by their services. The self-evaluation questionnaire also asks providers to add new indicators, which has proven critical in the past in order to motivate providers to use the tool. After providers reply to the whole questionnaire, the criteria are examined in order to obtain an overview of the current state of the quality of the institution, and a number of follow-up actions are planned to improve the situation if needed. Importantly, for each follow-up action providers need also to designate a responsible person in the team and set a deadline.

Although with some initial difficulties in ensuring buy-in by stakeholders, nowadays BRUK is used as a quality tool by both the providers themselves and the external evaluators of educational quality in Sweden. Importantly for the whole sector, the BRUK initiative helped introduce a common language and a common framework on quality in adult learning.

Evaluations by external bodies as an hybrid tool

An alternative strategy to monitor and evaluate the performance of training providers relies on external bodies to assess quality through inspections. External evaluations of this type are similar to self-evaluations in their functioning but they resemble certifications in their approach, since they are typically made mandatory for providers in order to access public funds.

In Norway, for example, the agency for lifelong learning (*SkillsNorway*) is in charge of the inspections of adult learning provided in Study Associations[2] and under the publicly funded training programme for basic working life skills (*SkillsPlus*). The aim of the *SkillsPlus* initiative is to give adults the opportunity to acquire the basic skills they need to keep up with the demands and changes in modern working life and civil society. Funding and participation have increased every year since the programme was established in 2006. The number of participants who have received training now exceeds 30 000. The programme concentrates on reading, writing, numeracy, and digital skills, and, since 2014, it also includes oral communication. Any enterprise in Norway, private and public, can apply for funding if they follow three criteria: (i) the learning activity should be combined with work and basic skills training should preferably be linked to other job-relevant learning; (ii) the courses should strengthen the participants' motivation to go on learning; and (iii) the courses have to relate to the competence goals approved by the Ministry of Education and Research. The providers – both public and private, as well as study associations – are important stakeholders in the programme, and they often write the applications on behalf of the enterprises or in their own right. In order to ensure quality of the *SkillsPlus* programme, *SkillsNorway* frequently undertakes inspections of the training providers. A negative finding from an inspection can result in an order to make changes, but also in withdrawal of public funding and/or an obligation to pay back received public funding.

In England, the Office for Standards in Education, Children's Services and Skills (OFSTED) undertakes inspections at all levels of formal education and training, including children's services, schools and academies, further education colleges, initial teacher training, youth work, work-based learning and adult education. OFSTED grades training providers based on their overall effectiveness, with a focus on: i) the effectiveness of leadership and management; ii) the quality of teaching, learning and assessment; iii) personal development, behaviour and welfare; and iv) outcomes for learners. Inspection judgements are based primarily on first-hand evidence gathered during on-site inspections, but inspectors also consult a range of publicly available data on learners' and apprentices' progress and achievement, and have access to a wide range of other information (including self-assessment reports of the providers). The criteria used by inspectors are laid out in the Further Education and Skills Inspection Handbook. Independent training providers who are judged to be inadequate will generally no longer receive funding from the Education and Skills Funding Agency. For Further Education colleges a negative review will lead to the development of a notice to improve, which sets out the conditions that the college must meet in a time bound period in order to receive continued funding.

The role of guidelines and other support materials to facilitate evaluations

Measuring the quality of training is challenging, even for training providers themselves, as quality is multi-dimensional and often subjective. Training providers can therefore benefit from support in implementing quality measures and systems for monitoring and evaluation. This type of support is available in some countries in the form of guidelines, criteria and quality standards, or support materials for training providers, such as good practice examples and self-evaluation tools.

Guidelines, criteria and quality standards can form the basis of a framework against which to evaluate the quality of training. Providing training organisations with guidelines will help them understand what is considered high-quality training provision and how it is measured. For example, training accredited by the Department for Adult Training (*Service de la Formation des Adultes*) in Luxembourg has to follow quality criteria in the areas of i) equal access, ii) transparency, and iii) trained teachers. Offering training providers access to support materials can also help them develop their quality systems. In Italy, the group involved in the Action Plan for Innovation in Adult Learning (PAIDEIA) disseminates good practices in terms of quality among training providers. In Finland, on top of carrying out evaluations, the Finnish Education Evaluation Centre (FINEEC) is tasked with supporting education and training providers in issues related to evaluation and quality assurance. In this respect, the centre formulates evaluation methods and indicators that education providers can use in self-evaluation and peer reviews. FINEEC also supports the development of an evaluation culture among education and training providers and promotes the spreading of good practices (OECD, 2019[3]).

In Ireland, the independent public body Quality and Qualifications Ireland (QQI) has the mandate of promoting quality and accountability in further education and training. Its main tool is a set of different quality assurance guidelines, that includes both a list of common core guidelines that are targeted to all providers and additional sector-specific guidelines for certain areas. In additional, QQI also has the role of disseminating other organisations' best practices, since they collaborate with a large range of adult training stakeholders.

In Slovenia, good practices, tools and recommendations are made available on an online platform (*Mozaik Kakovosti*) with the goal of providing support for training providers who are developing an internal quality system. Providers that take part in the Offering Quality Education to Adults (OQEA) initiative carry out planned, systematic and regular assessments and evaluations of their quality. At the beginning of each self-evaluation cycle, the organisation decides in which areas and with which indicators the self-evaluation will take place.

In Denmark, the Ministry of Children and Education does not directly impose the use of a particular quality assurance system to providers of adult training. While formal education institutions are required to have an evaluation system, providers of non-formal adult education are left to tackle quality issues as they deem satisfying. To help providers assess their overall quality, the Danish Adult Education Association (*Dansk Folkeoplysnings Samvirke*) – in collaboration with the Danish Evaluation Institute (*Danmarks Evalueringsinstitut*) – developed a tool for self-evaluation that is focused specifically on quality developments in non-formal education.[3] The process revolves around identifying and establishing in each organisation six main quality parameters, concerning:

- Teacher/Instructor/Activity leader
- Physical environment
- Communication
- Content
- Organisation
- Participant

The tool distinguishes between three steps. First, providers need to describe their practices and the concrete workflow of their organisation. Second, providers evaluate their practices, define their strengths and weaknesses, and identify what is important to maintain and what should improve. The third step aims at developing the provider's workflow for the future, based on the findings gathered from the previous phases. It is important that, regardless of whether the ultimate goals are minor or major, they remain realistic within the given organisational framework. Providers should also make sure to start with the most important parts first, lay out a specific plan of action, and set a specific date for evaluation. In addition to being very simple, the tool has two other advantages: providers can establish their own timeline and the consideration necessary to reflect on the issues at hand, and the model is adaptable to any organisation, regardless of structure, size or purpose.

Danish providers of adult labour market training (including non-formal ones) have also access to another self-evaluation tool (*VisKvalitet*) to help measure participants' satisfaction and learning outcomes, as well as the satisfaction of employers whose employees have participated in training programmes. The use of the *VisKvalitet* tool is now voluntary for continuing vocational education and training providers but was compulsory before 2014. The participant questionnaire includes: 10 common questions for unemployed participants and 12 for employed participants (e.g. "How much do you agree on the statement that the teaching was well planned?" and "Has this course meant that you can better take on new tasks in your workplace if needed?"); 3 background questions (e.g. "Whose idea was it for you to enrol in this course?" and "What is your education level?"); and the possibility of elaborating answers at the end of the evaluation.

Moreover, the tool gives flexibility to training providers to add personalised questions in addition to the mandatory ones. The employer questionnaire, in contrast, includes: four common questions (e.g. "To what extent does the course meet the needs of the company?" and "Would you recommend this course to others?"); and four background questions (e.g. "What was the reason for the employee to attend the course?").

An important step for an effective quality assurance system is also to build the capacity of staff in adult training institutions to have a good understanding of what quality is and how to monitor and assess it. In Slovenia, a training programme was developed by the Slovenian Institute for Adult Education (SIAE) for individuals to become quality counsellors in adult education. Training providers who want to improve their quality management system can have one or more staff members participate in the training or hire a qualified quality counsellor.

Quality awards and prizes

Rather than adopting certification, quality label systems, or external evaluations, some European countries rely on awards and prizes to develop a quality culture in the adult learning sector. For example, in Finland, the Ministry of Education and Culture organises a yearly quality award competition for adult education providers with the objective of encouraging learning centres to assess and continuously improve the quality of their activities. The rationale behind the initiative is to identify best practices that providers across the country can emulate, and to promote the overall value, attractiveness and visibility of the adult education sector. The Quality Award recognises the quality of services, continuous improvement and results, and exemplary work in the development of vocational training. The award of the prize is based on performance evaluation on predefined criteria determined by an expert committee appointed by the Ministry. A maximum of four quality awards are given each year, with the possibility of honourable mentions of merit in a specific theme, which is varies each year. For instance, in 2017 the theme was knowledge management, in 2018 it was the well-being of students and staff, while the 2020 theme was the holistic nature of quality management.[4] The amount of the prize is intended to be used to develop the activities of the training provider.

A similar initiative exists in Sweden, where a Quality Prize has been established by the so-called School Act of 2010. All kinds of schools can participate in the competition, including municipal adult education, as long as they document their actions towards quality improvements. The goal of the award is again motivating and inspiring schools to put in place quality-control processes.

References

Broek, S. and B. Buiskool (2013), *Developing the adult learning sector: Quality in the Adult Learning Sector*. [2]

OECD (2019), *Getting Skills Right: Future-Ready Adult Learning Systems*, Getting Skills Right, OECD Publishing, Paris, https://dx.doi.org/10.1787/9789264311756-en. [3]

OECD (2018), *Skills Strategy Implementation Guidance for Slovenia: Improving the Governance of Adult Learning*, OECD Skills Studies, OECD Publishing, Paris, https://dx.doi.org/10.1787/9789264308459-en. [4]

Slovenian Institute of Adult Education (2013), *Quality indicators in adult education*. [1]

Notes

[1] In Slovenia, there are approximately 500 providers of non-formal adult education and training (OECD, 2018[4]).

[2] The provision of non-formal adult education in Norway is handled by the so-called Study Associations (or Adult Education Associations). Their main objective is to provide educational opportunities that are independent of curricula and exams. Their courses cover a large number of activities, from purely leisure activities to vocational courses and academic subjects. There are currently 15 Study Associations, with group over 450 member organisations. In 2015, around 508 000 participants were registered at study association courses.

[3] https://www.daea.dk/themes/other-themes/ensuring-quality-in-non-formal-adult-education/.

[4] https://www.oph.fi/fi/koulutus-ja-tutkinnot/ammatillisen-koulutuksen-laatupalkinnot.

4 Ensuring quality in adult learning through additional support structures

Ensuring the quality of the adult education sector requires a holistic approach. Certification and evaluation of providers of adult learning are a necessary but not sufficient condition to ensure the highest possible quality of the sector. Validation of prior learning and lifelong guidance are central to the quality of adult education since they enable access, participation and progression, which are all intrinsic to quality in the field. Similarly, the professionalisation of the teaching staff is paramount to improve the overall quality of the adult education system, especially in the non-formal sector. Involving the social partners in quality assurance is also key to make sure that all stakeholders are fully involved in the (re)training of adults. Finally, information on quality should be publicised so that prospective learners, employers and institutions can make informed choices about which training to invest in.

Validation of prior learning and lifelong guidance

By definition, quality assurance represents all "activities involving planning, implementation, evaluation, reporting, and quality improvement, implemented to ensure that all education and training (content of programmes, curricula, assessment and validation of learning outcomes, etc.) meet the quality requirements expected by stakeholders" (Cedefop, 2011[11]). As such, validation of prior learning – i.e. the process of confirmation by an authorised body that an individual has acquired learning outcomes measured against a relevant standard (European Commission, 2013[2]) – becomes a critical element in the quality of adult training in terms of motivation, access, persistence and progression. Over the past few years, this has become more and more important given the increasingly heterogeneous nature of adult learning with its multiple and flexible upskilling pathways. Consequently, participants to the 2013 Thematic Working Group on quality in adult learning of the European Commission unanimously agreed that the availability of guidance and validation is an indispensable dimension of quality assurance of adult education and should form part of quality criteria for the certification of providers (European Commission, 2013[2]).

In fact, adults may have low qualification levels, but may have gained skills through years of work-experience that are equivalent to those associated with formal qualifications. Equally, while many adults may have low literacy and numeracy levels, they might nevertheless possess a range of other valuable skills such as the ability to drive different vehicles or care for customers (OECD, 2019[3]). Recognising these skills through validation and certification can benefit individuals, employers and the economy. For the individual, the validation recognises their (informal) learning effort, which can increase motivation and become a stepping-stone to further (formal) learning. Employers benefit from skill recognition through higher productivity, by being able to better match employees' skillsets and jobs. The benefits of skill validation and certification for the individual and employer, in turn, improve labour market functioning by making actual skills possessed by adults more visible to prospective employers (Kis and Windisch, 2018[4]). Overall, for these positive effects to materialise, it is important that employers and society at large value certificates that are obtained through skill recognition and see them as equivalent to those acquired through formal learning.

Although there is no unique approach to the recognition of existing skills and the recognition processes vary widely across contexts, they often include four phases: (1) identification of the experiences of an individual through dialogue; (2) documentation to support the individual's experiences; (3) a formal assessment of these experiences; and (4) certification of the results of the assessment which may lead to a partial or full qualification (cf. Council Recommendation of 20 December 2012 on the validation of non-formal and informal learning, 2012/C 398/01).

There is a clear link between validation and lifelong guidance, since learners need the guidance to embark on a validation pathway. For instance, in Portugal, *Qualifica Centres* are comprehensive one-stop shops for guidance on lifelong learning. The centres target adults with low qualifications, the unemployed and young people not in employment, education or training. One of the main responsibilities of the centres is the skills recognition, which is embedded in their overall guidance offer. Any adult seeking advice at one of the 303 *Qualifica Centres* undergoes a standardised four-step process: i) information and enrolment; ii) analysis and development of a skill profile; iii) discussion and definition of appropriate education and training path; and iv) referral to recognition procedures or appropriate education and training provision. To enter the recognition procedures, adults must be older than 18 years of age and have a minimum of 3 years professional experience. The process entails the preparation of a skill portfolio and a written, oral or practical exam. A jury awards a certificate of total or partial recognition. Partial recognition can lead to full recognition through the completion of modular training, although local provision may vary and not always be in line with the identified training needs. In 2017, 28 804 adults enrolled in recognition procedures and 10 157 received a certificate.

France has a long-standing tradition of recognising and certifying existing skills (*Validation des acquis de l'expérience* – VAE), which was strengthened by a 2002 law establishing the National Certification

Register, a dedicated commission which validates the conformity of certificates awarded through VAE. Adults can now gain recognition for around 1 300 qualifications by demonstrating that they have the relevant skills through work experience. Different bodies are responsible for implementing VAE, and various laws, decrees and frameworks ensure consistency between procedures.

The validation procedure has been described as demanding and lengthy, in particular for adults with low skills (Mathou, 2019[5]). For example, adults must not only be able demonstrate their previous experience in their written skill portfolio, but also be able to verbalise and reflect on their experience in a jury interview panel. In recent years, however, access to the recognition procedure has been made more inclusive for adults with low qualification levels and employers are now obliged to inform their employees about VAE every two years in the context of their professional development. Moreover, since late 2014, adults have the right to receive support during the VAE process, including in the preparation of the portfolio and interview process. In practice, the support is provided by the responsible bodies awarding the qualification or specific counselling providers. Adults also have access to specific VAE leave. The state also pays the cost of validation for unemployed people. For employees, the cost is covered by rights accumulated throughout working life. There is a mix of funding for 'in-between' cases; otherwise, the individual pays between EUR 600-2000. Yet, in spite of these changes, participation in the VAE has remained relatively constant in the past 13 years, and – if anything – it has decreased since 2014: around 25 000 complete certifications are delivered each year, with less than 24 000 in 2018 (French Ministry of Public Actions and Accounts, 2019[6]).

Over the last few years, more and more countries in Europe have attempted to develop quality assurance mechanisms specific to validation processes. For instance, according to Cedefop (2019[7]), the number of countries with explicit quality assurance arrangements for validation of prior learning has more than doubled, from 6 countries in 2014 to 15 in 2018. This implies that, in gradually more and more countries, any general quality assurance mechanism developed for the overall adult learning sector should co-habit with quality assurance systems specific to validation. Moreover, it is also important that any attempt to create a quality framework for the whole adult learning sector also ensures good coordination with career guidance services, in order to guarantee the most effective support to individuals' career decisions and personal development (Cedefop, 2019[8]).

Improving the quality of the teaching staff to improve the quality of the training

The professionalisation of the teaching staff is one of the most challenging aspects of quality assurance in adult education. Indeed, unlike in compulsory schooling and higher education, where the need for initial and continuous training as a teacher is less questioned, in adult learning there appears to be an assumption that, since a lot of non-formal learning is job-related, teachers' work experience is more valuable than their pedagogical skills (Broek and Buiskool, 2013[9]). Staff trained to teach at different levels are often hired to teach adults without upskilling in adult-specific teaching methodologies. However, the frequent non-formal dimension of adult learning creates a need to carefully balance the advantages of professionalisation with the potential drawbacks of over-regulation and over-burdening.

In many OECD countries, high-level qualification requirements exist to enter the adult learning sector, but they mostly apply only to formal learning. Exploiting information from ad hoc national reports, in 2009 the UNESCO Institute for Lifelong Learning collected data on the training qualifications required for adult education personnel in several OECD countries (Unesco Institute for Lifelong Learning (UIL), 2009[10]). As Table 4.1 shows, a secondary education qualification gives access to jobs as an adult trainer in only a few OECD countries. This is the case in Mexico, for example, where trainers simply need to have a junior high-school diploma and an inclination to teach. In the vast majority of countries, postgraduate qualifications are required, as well as a certain number of years of experience. However, these requirements do not typically apply to non-formal training. For instance, in Slovenia, adult educators in the formal sector must have a higher education qualification in the appropriate field and must pass a professional examination, while teachers in non-formal programmes of adult education are not bound to these requirements.

Moreover, even when countries require higher education qualifications, a university degree does not guarantee that trainers have the competencies to teach a public of adults. Requirements on teaching methods adapted to adults are virtually inexistent in most OECD countries. Only a few country require specific training in andragogic methods – among these, Estonia and Ireland are prominent examples.

Table 4.1. Qualifications and training levels of adult education personnel

Country	Area of training	Qualification – Entry	Qualification – Training
Austria	Adult Education	Different previous educational backgrounds, mainly depending on the provider sector	Universities and other institutions have didactically-oriented programmes for trainers and lecturers in their programme
Belgium (Flanders)	Adult Education	Since 2008 teachers in adult basic education need proof of pedagogical competence	Training of trainers programme, consisting of 280 teaching periods, 120 of which are dedicated to practical training
Denmark	Adult Education	Master's programme at a university or corresponding level; completion of a course in educational theory and practice	N/A
Estonia	Adult Education	Adult educators' professional qualification has four levels	N/A
Finland	Adult Education	Same qualification requirements as for teachers: degree in the teaching subject, 35 credit points in pedagogic studies (one credit point equal to 40 hours of student's work)	On average, Finnish teachers participate in continuing professional training for 9-15 days a year
Ireland	Adult Education	Qualifications for adult education organisers and coordinators employed by Vocational Education Committees are growing. For example, the NALA/WIT Higher Certificate in Arts in Adult Education (NFQ Level 6) or equivalent is required to become an Adult Literacy Organiser	In-service support and training is administered by the Department of Education and Science's Teacher Training Unit, the Further Education Support Service and a grant to the Vocational Education Committees is provided towards training in specific programmes
Slovak Republic	Adult Education	In general, university education in the field in which the educators lecture, practice in the field and the lecturer's skills constitute the basic requirement	N/A
Slovenia	Adult Education	Adult educators must have a higher education qualification in the appropriate field and must pass the professional examination; teachers in non-formal programmes of adult education are not bound to these demands	Teachers can receive at least five days of training per year or 15 days every three years
	Literacy	Literacy teachers must have a University degree, need to have finished adult education training and must pass the professional exam	Initial adult literacy teacher training is a 112- to 132-hour programme
Switzerland	Vocational Education and Training	The modular train-the-trainer system comprises four stages, each of which leads to a certificate or diploma which is required for an adult educator	N/A
United Kingdom	Further Education	Teaching qualification based on National Standards for teaching and supporting learning	N/A
Israel	Adult Education	Teacher's college or university certification is a prerequisite for employment in publicly administered adult education; facilitators require certification by the Division of Adult Education	Participation in periodic in-service training sessions is part of the accepted timetable of teachers
Australia	Vocational Education and Training	National certificate in training and assessment	N/A
	Literacy	Teaching qualification and postgraduate qualification with at least three years' experience	N/A

Country	Area of training	Qualification – Entry	Qualification – Training
New Zealand	Literacy	Specific qualifications for adult literacy and numeracy educators have recently been developed, including a qualification for educators engaged in other vocational learning	N/A
Korea	Adult Education	Lifelong educators are certified by the government. They are neither subject masters nor instructors	Training through undergraduate, graduate courses, or in-service course programmes
Chile	Adult Education	Same requirements as required to practise as a teacher in the school system, namely a university degree	Courses of one week, followed by annual refresher sessions
Mexico	Adult Education	15 years-old or older, must have fulfilled junior high studies, an inclination to teach and availability to travel	The permanent training of these facilitators most cover three stages: orientation, initial training and continuing education

Source: UIL (2009[10]), Global report on adult learning and education, https://unesdoc.unesco.org/ark:/48223/pf0000186431.

For these reasons, several countries have recently put in place specific projects to improve the quality of the teaching staff of adult learning programmes. For instance, since training for teaching staff in adult education is not regulated in Switzerland, instructors have frequently been working in voluntary or part-time positions without professional training. To solve this problem, following the recent rise in interest in the qualifications of adult trainers, the Swiss Federation for Adult Learning (SVEB) in 1995 introduced the programme "Train the Trainer" (AdA). AdA is a 3-level core concept of staff quality, which provides a 3-level certificate of the competences of adult education instructors.

In a similar vein, Austria established its Academy of Continuing Education (WBA) in 2007 as a validation system for the qualification and recognition of adult educators. The WBA is aimed at individuals from one of the four main professions in adult education who are actively involved in adult education in Austria, namely managerial positions, teaching and training, career guidance and counselling, and librarianship. The Academy recognises adult educators' qualifications according to set standards based on qualification profiles, and it acknowledges prior learning results and offers guidance and counselling for the acquisition of missing skills. It does not offer further education programmes itself but accredits suitable courses offered by various adult education institutions throughout Austria. It awards two degrees: a certificate of basic competences in all four fields of adult education, and a higher-level diploma based on the certificate but focusing on the specific field the educators want to specialise in.

In Slovenia, the Institute for Adult Education provides professional training for adult educators with a threefold objective: i) acquire new knowledge and skills in order to perform quality work; ii) share their experience with others and evaluate their own practices under expert guidance in order to improve them; and iii) rethink their own professional identity of adult educator by professionally connecting with others. Three types of programmes are offered: (1) in the *general basic training* programme, participants acquire and further develop the knowledge of the discipline of adult education; (2) in the *basic training for special roles* programme, participants acquire basic knowledge for performing special roles, such as mentor in study circles, counsellor in guidance centres, quality counsellor, etc.; and (3) in the *further training* programme, participants upgrade their knowledge and reflect on their practice. Importantly, the Slovenian Institute for Adult Education allows recognition of prior learning for teachers. An up-to-date website contains all the information on activities, programmes and events organised by the Institute (https://izobrazevanje.acs.si/).

The European Commission has also provided guidance on teacher training in adult learning. In 2013, a Thematic Working Group on quality in adult learning of the European Commission developed a policy checklist in order to provide public authorities with a tool to self-assess existing policies, structures and systems for quality assurance of adult learning staff (European Commission, 2013[2]). The checklist covers: i) legal regulations for the qualifications of adult learning staff; ii) regulatory frameworks for the professional development of staff; iii) career paths/pathways leading to the profession; iv) the employment situation of adult learning staff; v) data collection for policy development; vi) systematic and regular promotion of the nature and benefits of adult learning professions; and vii) quality assurance and quality management. By gathering information under a detailed list of sub-headings on the above areas, the results of such an assessment aim at helping governments identifying gaps in their national framework for the professionalisation of adult trainers. In addition to the checklist on staff quality, the Thematic Working Group also elaborated a preliminary profiling grid for adult learning staff. Using the grid, providers themselves can self-evaluate the key competences required by staff working in the various sub-domains of adult learning. Overall, the aim is to show how different competences have different degrees of importance in different sectors. Creating teacher profiles could support providers in developing training for under-qualified staff and at the same time be in a position to offer validation of non-formal and informal learning to experienced staff lacking a professional qualification to teach adults.

Involving the social partners in quality assurance

The social partners can be involved in quality assurance at different levels, through providing oversight on boards of education providers, as part of local or sectoral quality assurance bodies or having representation on national agencies responsible for the quality assurance of adult learning (OECD, 2019[11]). Indeed, in some countries, the social partners have a role in agencies that ensure the quality of (parts of) the adult learning system. For instance, the Swedish National Agency for Higher Vocational Education (*Myndigheten för yrkeshögskolan*) ensures the quality of higher vocational education programmes, and its advisory council for labour market issues comprises both trade unions and employers. The role of the advisory council includes the inspections of providers and programmes, including work-based training elements. The inspections entail observational visits, interviews with students, tutors, teachers and head coordinators. Based on the inspection, as well as an assessment of labour market needs, the council advises the National Agency about which training programmes should receive state grants and be included in the higher vocational education offer (Kuczera, 2013[12]).

Similarly, the social partners in Denmark are involved in the 11 continuing training and education committees, which monitor adult vocational training in different sectors of the labour market. One of the key inputs to the monitoring of programmes and providers is information produced through the system *VisKvalitet*. As discussed above, this system collects data from each participant about their satisfaction with the training via a questionnaire, as well as data from a sample of companies whose employees have attended training. Results are used by the committees to identify quality issues and develop remedial action.

The social partners can also be involved in the certification of adult learning providers: Flanders (Belgium) is currently introducing changes to their certification system to guarantee that training corresponds to labour market needs. Since September 2019, there are three certification streams for adult learning programmes that benefit from government funding: i) automatic certification for some training programmes (often more general or formal), such as the ones provided through adult education centres and higher education institutions; ii) certification through the social partners (*Paritaire Comités*) for training organised at the sector level; and iii) certification by the Flemish certification commission (*Vlaamse erkenningscommissie*) for all other training. The certification commission consists of the social partners.

Many countries have complex multi-level quality assurance systems, which are supported by the social partners. In Germany, for example, certification of training programmes in the context of active labour market policies is conducted by certifying bodies (*Zertifizierungsstelle*). One of the better-known certifying bodies, CERTQUA, is run by the leading German employer organisations. Certifying bodies, in turn, need to be accredited by the German Federal Public Employment Agency (*Bundesagentur für Arbeit*). An advisory council supports the agency in this work. Trade unions and employer organisations are part of the council.

Publicising information on providers' quality

For individuals, employers and institutions to be able to make informed choices about which training to invest in, they need to have access to relevant and up-to-date information on the quality of different training providers and programmes. Certification and quality labels can serve as signals of quality, but training providers can also share more in-depth information on evaluations, learning outcomes and user satisfaction with the general public to help them decide which training to invest in. This information should ideally be easily accessible, presented in a user-friendly format. Indeed, consumer protection is an important objective of quality assurance systems.

In some countries, quality assurance bodies make the results from evaluations publicly available. In Norway, for example, *Skills Plus* makes the results from inspections of *Skills Plus* programmes and adult training in Study Associations available on its website. In the United Kingdom, the Department for Education publishes summary tables of outcome-based success measures, including sustained employment and learning rates, by provider on its website. In France, certain public institutions that finance training have to review the quality of the training providers they work with, and make the outcomes from the review process publicly available. For training providers that do not hold a specific quality label, the review consists of an evaluation of six quality criteria, including education and training of teachers and sharing of information on training outcomes. Training providers that comply with the criteria are registered in an online database accessible to financers of training (*DataDock*).

In some of those countries that make use of self-evaluation systems, it is actually compulsory to make the results publicly available. For example, in Denmark, the results from self-evaluations through the national *VisKvalitet* tool are centralised and published online. To protect learners' data privacy, answers to the questionnaire are publicly shown only when at least 35 participants have answered. The system provides many opportunities to compare and track developments over time, both for individual labour market education and for schools. Box 4.1 shows how even countries outside Europe, such as Korea and Australia, share information on quality of adult training through online databases.

Box 4.1. Sharing information on quality through online databases: Evidence from outside Europe

Online databases that provide details on existing training programmes can help individuals, employers and institutions make informed adult learning choices. In some cases, these databases also provide quality information, such as learning outcomes or user satisfaction. The Korean HRD-Net website provides a wealth of information for a wide range of different training programmes. In addition to basic information on the duration of the course, the costs and the average age of the participants, the website also provides information on the employment rate and average wages of the graduates from the programmes. It also shows the satisfaction of participants, on a range from zero to five stars, and their reviews. Australia's national directory of vocational education and training providers and courses (www.myskills.gov.au) allows users to search VET qualifications by industry and access information about average course fees, course duration, available subsidies and average employment outcomes. While employment outcomes are currently available by qualification, a plan exists to make them available at the provider level.

Source: OECD (2019[13]), *Getting Skills Right: Future-Ready Adult Learning Systems*, https://dx.doi.org/10.1787/9789264311756-en.

References

Broek, S. and B. Buiskool (2013), *Developing the adult learning sector: Quality in the Adult Learning Sector.*   [9]

Cedefop (2019), *Coordinating guidance and validation*, http://dx.doi.org/10.2801/801290.   [8]

Cedefop (2019), *European inventory on validation of non-formal and informal learning 2018.*   [7]

Cedefop (2011), *Glossary: Quality in education and training*, Cedefop, Luxembourg, http://dx.doi.org/10.2801/94487.   [1]

European Commission (2013), *Thematic Working Group on Quality in Adult Learning Final Report.*   [2]

French Ministry of Public Actions and Accounts (2019), *Annexe au projet de loi de finances pour 2020 - Formation professionnelle*, https://www.ressources-de-la-formation.fr/doc_num_data.php?explnum_id=22115.   [6]

Kis, V. and H. Windisch (2018), "Making skills transparent: Recognising vocational skills acquired through workbased learning", *OECD Education Working Papers*, No. 180, OECD Publishing, Paris, https://dx.doi.org/10.1787/5830c400-en.   [4]

Kuczera, M. (2013), *A skills beyond school commentary on Sweden*, OECD, Paris, http://www.oecd.org/education/skills-beyond-school/ASkillsBeyondSchoolCommentaryOnSweden.pdf (accessed on 19 May 2020).   [12]

Mathou, C. (2019), *2018 update to the European inventory on validation of non-formal and informal learning, Country Report France.*   [5]

OECD (2019), *Getting Skills Right: Engaging low-skilled adults in learning*, http://www.oecd.org/employment/emp/engaging-low-skilled-adults-2019.pdf (accessed on 19 May 2020).   [3]

OECD (2019), *Getting Skills Right: Future-Ready Adult Learning Systems*, Getting Skills Right, OECD Publishing, Paris, https://dx.doi.org/10.1787/9789264311756-en.   [13]

OECD (2019), *Getting Skills Right: Making adult learning work in social partnership*, http://www.oecd.org/employment/emp/adult-learning-work-in-social-partnership-2019.pdf.   [11]

Unesco Institute for Lifelong Learning (UIL) (2009), *Global report on adult learning and education.*, UNESCO Institute for Lifelong Learning, https://unesdoc.unesco.org/ark:/48223/pf0000186431 (accessed on 19 May 2020).   [10]

5 The Quality Assurance in Adult Learning Decision Tree

Developing a new quality assurance mechanism for non-formal adult learning involves numerous, often consecutive steps. The Quality Assurance in Adult Learning Decision Tree has been developed to help public authorities planning reform of their quality assurance systems make sure they take into consideration the most relevant decisions. These include: (1) whether the new mechanism should be mandatory for providers to operate or receive public funds; (2) what is the scope of the mechanism; (3) which instrument should be at the core of the new quality framework; (4) what are the characteristics of the instrument; (5) who does what; (6) whether additional support structures should be implemented; and (7) whether it is necessary to establish measures for a transition period.

A decision tree to establish a quality assurance system in adult learning

Overall, the available empirical evidence on the best quality assurance mechanisms in Europe is still too scarce in order to provide univocal recommendations for countries that are interested in embarking in the elaboration of a national quality assurance programme or reforming it to enhance quality. This is particularly the case in the context of non-formal adult learning with its mix of public and private interventions. Yet, this review of the current existing practices suggests that it is paramount to initiate a discussion about the quality of adult education, and that there exist several examples of successful initiatives at European level to draw inspiration from.

To assist public authorities that are considering improving or creating a quality assurance system for non-formal adult learning, the following decision tree aims at providing an overview of the factors that they need to consider in its design and implementation (Figure 5.1).

As discussed throughout the report, the first decision that the authorities need to make is to establish the approach they want to follow in creating the quality assurance system (Decision #1). The choice is between imposing rigid minimum quality standards that providers of adult training need to meet in order to operate or receive public funds (*regulatory approach*) or adopting non-binding guidelines to help providers improve the quality of their services (*advisory approach*). They then need to determine the scope of the intervention, and clarify whether they want the new mechanism to cover all providers of adult learning, or only a subset of them – for example only those delivering basic skills training, or only those accessing public funding, etc. (Decision #2).

Identifying the main instrument to operationalise the new quality assurance framework (Decision #3) and its characteristics (Decision #4) probably requires the greatest efforts, both in terms of time, coordination, and involvement of all relevant stakeholders. Elements to be taken into consideration when designing effective certifications, labels and evaluations are numerous and complex, and should be therefore planned with the aid of experts and academics. Moreover, as stressed by this review of European practices, the participation of all the key adult learning actors in this phase is crucial to ensure the buy-in of providers, social partners and local governments. More so if quality labels already exists.

In parallel of establishing the terms of the main instrument, the authorities have to figure out who will be in charge of the implementation and overall governance of the new quality assurance mechanism (Decision #5). European countries have used combinations of public, private and non-profit bodies, both at national and local levels. The decision clearly depends on the existing infrastructure in each country, and it may also involve the creation of a new ad-hoc body. Furthermore, this report has emphasised the importance of adopting a holistic approach to quality and the elaboration of a whole series of initiatives to support the development of a quality culture in adult learning. As such, governments are encouraged to think more broadly on what additional support structures should be put in place, based on their own national context, strengths and weaknesses (Decision #6). Finally, transition measures may have to be adopted to help the sector gradually adapt to the new quality assurance system and encourage the buy-in of the wider public (Decision #7).

Figure 5.1. The Quality Assurance in Adult Learning Decision Tree

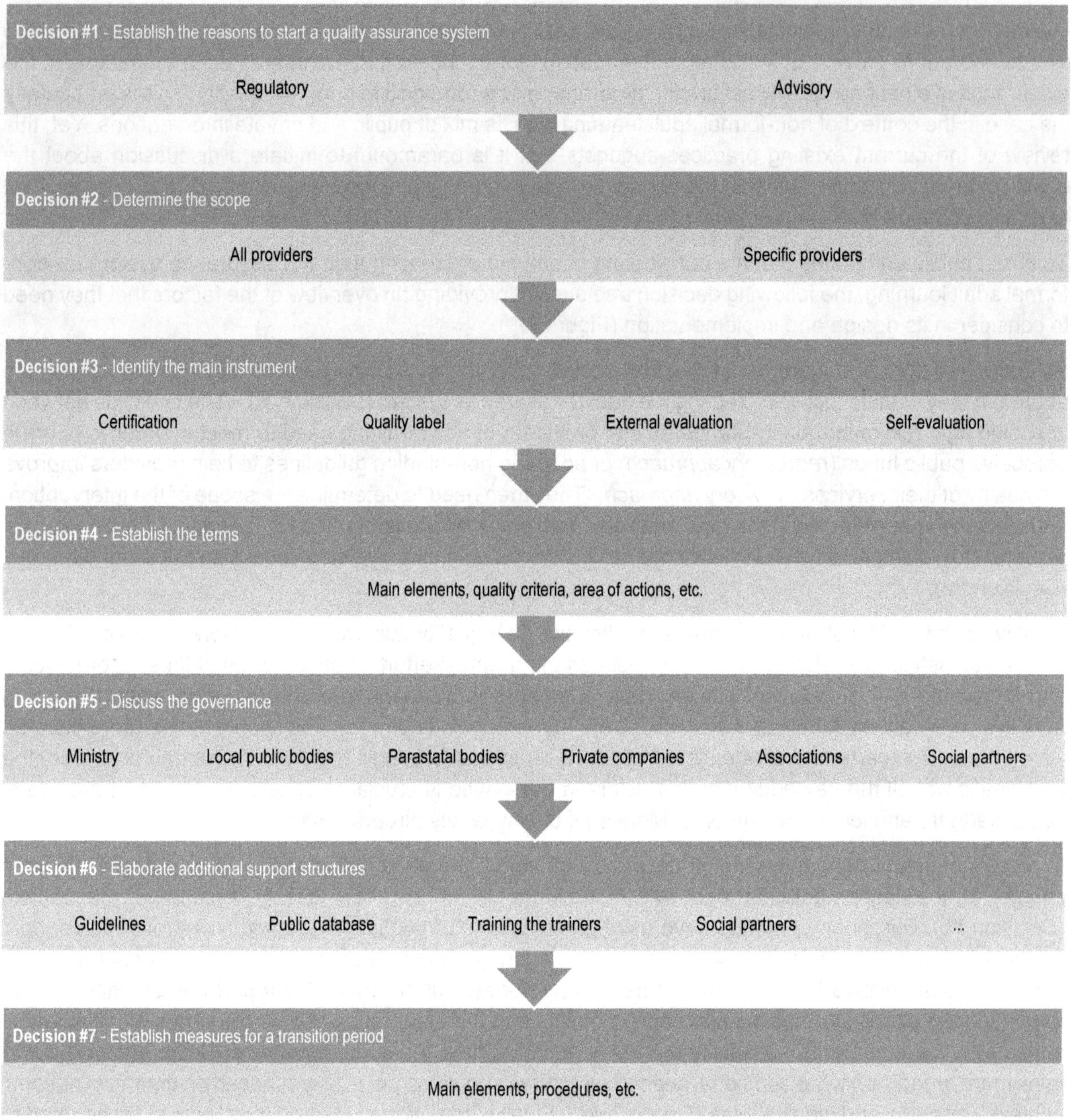

Decision #1 - Establish the reasons to start a quality assurance system

| Regulatory | Advisory |

Decision #2 - Determine the scope

| All providers | Specific providers |

Decision #3 - Identify the main instrument

| Certification | Quality label | External evaluation | Self-evaluation |

Decision #4 - Establish the terms

Main elements, quality criteria, area of actions, etc.

Decision #5 - Discuss the governance

| Ministry | Local public bodies | Parastatal bodies | Private companies | Associations | Social partners |

Decision #6 - Elaborate additional support structures

| Guidelines | Public database | Training the trainers | Social partners | ... |

Decision #7 - Establish measures for a transition period

Main elements, procedures, etc.

www.ingramcontent.com/pod-product-compliance
Lightning Source LLC
Chambersburg PA
CBHW051234200326
41519CB00025B/7376